OVER
3600
PERFECT PET NAMES

DOC, HIGGINS, JIGSAW, or PRUDENCE...

Great names for a Virgo pet or any critter who never tires of "stupid pet tricks," stays home without a fuss while you're away, and is a breeze to care for.

WOLF, BUDDY, BRIGETTE, SHADOW...

Simply *purr*fect monikers for the pet who appeared on your doorstep and adopted *you*! Chances are that that determined orphan is a Scorpio, and all too quickly stole your heart.

WIZARD, REBEL, SPARKY, or VALENTINE...

If your pet is "Human's Best Friend," loving you—and every other person it meets—it's probably an Aquarius who needs a name to fit its wonderfully wacky nature . . . or a name like ED, RUTH, GABRIELLE, or SCOT that says just how amazingly "human" this animal really is.

Plus special names for tandems and trios and 144 sign-by-sign pet/owner comparisons to help you trouble-shoot problems and choose the most compatible pet for you!

Pet Names

Names

Pet Signs

KAREN WEBSTER

A DELL BOOK

Published by
Dell Publishing
a division of
Bantam Doubleday Dell Publishing Group, Inc.
666 Fifth Avenue
New York, New York 10103

ISBN: 0-440-20477-1

Designed by Jeremiah B. Lighter

Printed in the United States of America
Published simultaneously in Canada

December 1989
10 9 8 7 6 5 4 3 2
OPM

For Robert and Lillian with love

ACKNOWLEDGMENTS

To my best buddy for daring me to act on my next idea. Life's been better for knowing you.

To Marilyn Wright for your generous and open-hearted support and encouragement.

To Andrew Shanley for being a true friend and coach. I couldn't have done it without you.

To Dr. Robert Williams and his wonderful secretary, Karen Clark, and to Dr. Gary Silverstein and his wonderful secretary, Amy Barr, for compiling and sharing their list of pet names.

To Missy, Eric, Rip, Fred, and Steve, who were forced to read this innumerable times for comment. Did I mention that I've already started on the next project?

To the memory of Cleo and Lujo, and the living technicolor of Kiera. Hasn't life been grand?

Contents

Prologue

When I was a young girl growing up in Woodbury, Connecticut, years before it became a fashionable bedroom community of New York City, pets were practically a necessity. There were acres and acres of fields and woods everywhere. If you didn't have a dog, horse, or some other four-legged creature tagging along (I had all of the above), it could get pretty lonely on those country excursions to visit with playmates. So I learned very early about the joys and the value of pet companionship. So much so that my first job was working for a veterinarian. I was hooked for life. To this day, given the choice of sharing an afternoon's drive with most adult humans or my dog, you'll find me wrapping the front seat of my car with an old army blanket.

My fondness for the four-leggeds may also be because I make my living talking to people, and in such an unusual and unorthodox way that people like to talk about me. For the past twelve years I've been a professional consultant who incorporates astrology as part of my services. I counsel people from

all walks of life, conduct seminars, lead workshops,
appear on radio and television, and all in all have
quite a successful career.

My puppy couldn't care less. Nor is she impressed that I've studied abroad and counseled big
shots and big businesses. She sees me as the rather
rambunctious and sometimes comical human that I
really am. At 3 A.M. I might be up pacing around my
office working on my next business project. By 5
A.M. I might be ready to go off for a long walk or a
cross-country ski with my pal at my heels before the
rest of the world is up and running. When we feel
the urge to act a little willy nilly, we don't spend
much time worrying over appearances; I jumped
that fence long ago.

That all sort of adds up to how this came to be
my first foray into the world of writing books. It
started as an idea that lighted on me as a humorous
interruption and some wishful thinking during one
of my late-night brainstorming sessions. I was trying to imagine a name for a much-longed-for pet
when I should have been putting the last touches on
a new seminar. My bold idea was to combine my
love for animals and my love for writing. (At the
time, I had neither a dog nor an editor.) Finally a
friend dared me to either put up or shut up.

So here it is. I've won my dare. Now I hope that
I can win your smile in my endeavor to amuse you
and provide you with some interesting though ad-
mittedly offbeat information about the wonderful
world of pets.

Which leads to the story of "Me and My Gal" or
how my new pet and this book, all in one fell swoop,
came to be. . . .

1

Where this book
came from

It was the first hot, sunny day after the snow melted. My neighbor's big black Labrador puppy had strayed over to my backyard while I was working in my garden. Rufus decided, after watching me for a while, that digging in the dirt looked like great fun. So he proceeded to join me. As I was painstakingly planting the peppers, he was enthusiastically digging up my tomato plants, all the while bashing me in the face with his tail, which was wagging in circles like helicopter blades. Naturally, I found all of this so endearing that I ran right out and bought my very own puppy.

Getting my pet safely home was not an easy task. This was her very first car ride. When we started off she was neatly tucked inside her carrying box, but this tidy arrangement lasted all of fifteen minutes. Her woeful whimpering won out. I opened the top just enough so she could see me. That was all the invitation she needed. Waiting for the opportune moment when I had to shift gears— quicker than you could say *boo*—she scrambled out

and plopped herself unceremoniously on my lap.
For the rest of the trip, worn out by her supreme
effort, she could manage only to hang her head out
the window or drool on my blouse.

Half an hour later we pulled into the driveway.
"We're home," I announced with an encouraging
look. She wobbled her first few steps out of the car
and collapsed in a panting heap by the back porch. I
guess she figured that after all she'd been through
up to this point, the stairs were a no-go.

So there we were looking at each other. Me,
gazing down at her, wondering what she'd be like
when she grew up, and if we'd be as close as I'd been
with my last pet, she looking up at me, one ear
flopped over, wondering why I'd taken her away
from her last remaining brother and sister. I think
we both concluded that we'd just have to wait and
see. Once inside, I got her a bowl of water and myself a glass of tea. "Here's to a long and happy fu-
ture together," I toasted, detecting a faint wag of
her tail.

A few things were still conspiring to disturb my
newfound bliss. First and foremost, what was I going to call this furry round ball with a wet nose, and
a floppy ear? No name popped magically into my
head. Alas, my normally quick wit was failing me.
The more I tried to think of a clever or appropriate
name, the more nothing came. I'd used up all my
most favorite names, it seemed, on previous pets. I
was not about to stoop to something such as Charlie
Jr. or Charles the Third. It was going to be an origi-
nal, or nothing. And nothing was unacceptable.

And then I start thinking—what have I done?
I've got this . . . this little bundle, who's going to

turn into a very big bundle, and I know virtually nothing about her likes or dislikes, her tendencies or traits, or even what makes her unique to her species. And what if she grows up and doesn't even like me?

Not one to stay stumped for long, I decided to run to the bookstore to look for some help. Surely someone else before me had pondered these weighty matters. But, nope, I couldn't turn up much of anything. Oh yes, there were books on what to feed your pet (no problem—Purina took care of that for me), and how to groom your pet (no problem—I've got an old dog brush that will do the trick), and all the accessories you could buy, including diamond-studded leashes, raincoats, beds, houses, and so on (no problem—my puppy was not going to be raised as a yuppie).

Big problem—no books on pet names, and no books on astrology to give me a clue to my buddy's personality or preferences. The scientific information that might have interested me was buried in a tome that must have weighed fifty pounds. Dejected, I returned home, mission failed.

As if sensing my troubled thoughts, my pet came over to greet me. She jumped up, licked my hand, and promptly tinkled on my leg. Well, I figured, at least she has a sense of humor. That's a good sign.

In that moment I had a revelation. I would create my own solution. I would write the very book I was looking for. This would kill two birds with one stone, or, for bird lovers, take the cat by the tail, or, for cat lovers, take the bull by the horns . . . (I don't know of any bull lovers, except maybe politicians, and I suspect they get their speechwriters to think up names—but I digress). By writing this book, I would find a name and a knowable identity for my beloved buddy, while entertaining myself and, I hope, you as well.

The research for this book took me on a rollicking romp through petdom. I found more than a few interesting traits common to pets and pet owners. Along with learning that there are thousands of sublime and ridiculous names for our mongrels and purebreds, my informal sociological survey also showed that we pet owners are particularly sentimental, easily amused, weird, perverse, inspired. I found as well that when it comes to picking our pets, your guess is as good as mine as to how we arrive at our final choices.

The intention of this book is to make that process more predictable and pleasant. Each chapter takes you through the natural stages of pet selection. If you're not sure what kind of pet you want, Chapter 2 illuminates the vast variety of pets from which you can choose, along with what makes each of them so special. Chapter 3 gives you, I must modestly say, the most comprehensive astrological guide to pets available today. It even includes a sign-by-sign analysis and comparison, so that you'll be sure to pick your perfect match. Chapter 4 offers an up-to-date and complete list of stellar pet names with over 3,600 entries. Chapter 5 concludes that our pets have also imparted names to us and notes some of the more vivid contributions that our pets have offered to the English language.

Finally, let me say that all pet owners do agree on one thing: The rewards of having a pet are great.

This book is a small token of my appreciation to all the wonderful pets who have enriched my life and to all the wonderful pets who will enrich yours. I hope you have as much fun reading it as I had writing it.

2

Categories of pet species

When most people hear the word pet, they immediately think of cats and dogs. This is certainly understandable; cats and dogs make great pets. They are also far and away the most frequently chosen pets. But it seems unfair to the rest of the animal kingdom who have offered their services, at one time or another, as faithful and loyal companions. I mean, who would Daniel be without his lion, or Jonah without his whale, or the Lone Ranger without Silver?

Down through history, there are numerous examples of pets who have performed heroic deeds and overcome incredible odds for their masters. Many stories are both touching and astounding. For example, for centuries dolphins have been regarded as the friends of seafarers. Sailors knew that when dolphins came around, they kept the sharks away. One particular recorded incident tells how a dolphin rescued a boy who had been washed overboard during a storm. The boy clung to the dolphin's back while it swam the several miles to shore, most certainly saving the boy's life.

Then there is the unknown, undocumented story of the man and his fly. A man moved to California, and, amid all the commotion of moving, he forgot to take his pet fly with him. It took this dedicated pet three months to make the harrowing cross-country journey. When the fly finally arrived, hungry and tired, he mustered his last strength to greet his friend by dive-bombing the screen door until he was indeed recognized as *the* very same pet fly from Connecticut. At last owner and pet were happily reunited.

Perhaps now you can see why I feel it is important to widen the horizon of prospective pet owners, to enlighten them regarding the myriad choices awaiting them. There are so many wonderful creatures waiting to cheer you with their company and delight you with their diverse personalities.

So, when we think about pets, let's acknowledge that practically every animal on the planet has been a pet for someone, somewhere, sometime. And once we've recognized the scope of our pet options, we can truly and forevermore see that there is a lot more to this pet business than Fido and Kitty.

Thus, when we start thinking about every goldarn animal on the planet, we had better talk about categories. To help in this potentially mind-boggling task, I will enumerate and discuss each of the classifications from whence pets have come. The importance of this categorizing, I must say, was sort of browbeaten into me by an old pal. Bradford, a brilliant zoologist who lives down the road, insists that

"If one wants to own a pet, one should act responsibly and become a little more informed about it than simply knowing its gender and age."

To humor Bradford and hopefully help you, I've noted a few facts and made a few observations about what makes your pet unique to its species. Included are some suggestions about the food, care, and housing needs, together with some of the advantages and disadvantages of the following categories of animal species: mammals, birds, reptiles, amphibians, fish, insects, and et ceteras. As the saying goes, "Forewarned is forearmed."

By the time you finish this chapter, you should know exactly which pet category will suit you and your lifestyle best. Then you and your chosen pet will have a much better chance of living happily ever after.

MAMMALS

Mammals are undoubtedly the most common category from which the average pet owner chooses a pet. Mammals are warm-blooded animals characterized by a four-chambered heart, a hinged backbone, hair or fur, the ability to nurse their young, and the need to breathe air. Of the million or so different kinds of animals that exist on earth, only about 4,300 species belong to this classification.

Mammals basically fall into two categories: meat-eaters and vegetarians. Richly varied, they come in a cornucopia of forms. They can be fishlike —whales and porpoises; lizardlike—certain marsupial mice; tortoiselike—armadillos; birdlike—flying bats; four-legged—horses and dogs; and last but not least, two-legged—man (who is, of course, the most difficult pet to housebreak).

Mammals range in size from a shrew, which can weigh as little as a nickel, to the blue whale, which can grow to 112 feet and weigh as much as 170 tons. (That translates to 340,000 pounds for you weight-conscious folks.)

Mammals, for the most part, have the run of the planet. You'll encounter them everywhere, in all environments. They set up house on the ground, in the air, in all bodies of water, from deserts to icecaps.

Because they are warm-blooded, mammals are quite adept at maintaining their body temperature in extreme heat or frigid cold. As their bodies have some form of insulation, mammals can survive in climates that would quickly send other animals to the Great Beyond.

Advantages

• Mammals are warm-blooded like you, so they can go anywhere you can go.

• You'll never have to eat leftovers again.

• It's easier to find a pet who will lavish you with unconditional love than a human.

- Mammals include cats and dogs, the most common and frequently owned pets. Owning one of them won't tip your neighbors off to any of your other peculiarities.

Disadvantages

- They often run off unless chained or trained.

- Their vet bills can rival your mortgage payments.

- They need a babysitter if you don't want to take them on vacation with you.

Housing

- Yours will do. Except of course for whales and elephants, in which case they are best left to their own housing. Barns are optional for horses, goats, and pigs.

Food

- Yours will do, though it's generally considered wiser, healthier, and cheaper to rely on a national-brand pet food.

Care

- Lots of TLC. The more you give, the more you get.

- Some studies would have us believe that it is the pets who really care for us and keep us healthy with their love, instead of the reverse. I figure any way you look at it—you love them more, they love you more—it's a good deal all the way around.

BIRDS

Birds are a fairly numerous group, with more than nine thousand varieties. It is somewhat remarkable, at least to my way of thinking, that they are distantly related to the quite larger, now-extinct dinosaurs. Because they can fly, they've settled themselves almost everywhere from the frozen polar caps, to the highest peaks of the Himalayas, to the steamy recesses of the tropical forests. Their ability to navigate and their reasons for migrating still puzzle man. I don't know why this is so. I think it makes perfect sense to winter in Florida.

Although all birds have beaks, some form of wings, and are hatched from eggs, not all birds can fly. (Witness the kiwi and the penguin.) And all birds have feathers, which makes them different from all other animals. If in doubt—Is it a bird? Is it a plane? Is it Superman?—this one trait is always a dead giveaway.

Birds range in size from the flightless ostrich—males of this species reach eight feet in height, weigh in at over 300 pounds, and run at speeds of up to 40 miles per hour—to the tiny bee hummingbird of only two inches, whose darting flight can reach

150 miles per hour with wings beating at 200 flaps per second.

Birds are also the only species in which some can be taught to mimic the human language. The best-known talkers are the yellow-headed parrots.

Advantages

- There's nothing more cheerful than having your own in-house chirpers and tweeters.

- They won't shed hair on your favorite chair.

- Their ethereal beauty and gentle presence are soothing to be around.

Disadvantages

- They don't like to sleep on your bed with you at night.

- They won't jog around the block with you.

- Their fallen birdseed shells take great delight in attacking the bottom of your bare feet, so it's advisable to vacuum daily.

- They don't have sphincter muscles. If you choose to let them fly freely about, everything is fair game.

Housing

- They prefer trees, but if you don't have any in your home, a birdcage will usually do.

Food

- Unless you have one of the carnivorous types who like mice and other rodents, birdseed is recommended. Also, if you are not in the habit of

making stuffing, your stale bread makes a tasty
treat for your feathered friend. Don't forget the
greens. (Lettuce is good.)

Care

- Unlike many other pets, birds do seem to enjoy
  being tucked in at bedtime. A blanket of sorts,
  placed over their cage at night, will help to protect them from drafts or the swatting paws of
  cats.

REPTILES

The reptiles—crocodiles, alligators, turtles, lizards, and snakes—are cold-blooded, egg-laying ver-
tebrates with scaly skin.

Technically speaking, the Age of Reptiles ended
65 million years ago with the exit of the dinosaurs.
But there are still several thousand leftover species
surviving today.

Turtles are the oldest type of living reptile.
There are about two hundred different kinds. The
crocodilians have about twenty species. Lizards and
snakes are the largest group, with around two thousand types.

As reptiles keep growing throughout their lives, though more slowly as they get older, it's hard to determine normal adult size and length. However, they are categorized into dwarf, medium-size, and gigantic species. (If you choose to own the gigantic species, it's a good idea to check your town zoning laws. Sad but true, prejudice still abounds when it comes to allowing twenty-foot crocodiles into the neighborhood.)

Reptiles are also noted for their longevity. The tortoise has been known to live for more than 175 years and the American alligator can live past 50.

Most people prefer to live and let live when it comes to this category. But if it does happen to be your pet of choice, you strange person, read on.

Advantages

- They make great conversation pieces.

- "Beware of Hungry Crocodile" has lots more punch than "Beware of Dog."

- If you have a turtle (the most common pet of the reptile group) and it decides to run away, you don't have to start chasing it until next Thursday.

- You don't have to worry about them overpopulating, as many have a tendency to eat their own young.

Disadvantages

- Having an affectionate boa constrictor who likes to give hugs.

- Having a color-blind alligator who can't tell the difference between your arm and its dinner.

- Having a chameleon who likes to play hide and seek. If you suddenly feel a goosh under your shoe, you've won the game (though there are those picky people who would say it was by default).

Housing

- Flat rocks with lots of sunshine.

Food

- Depending on which size and type of species you have, they will require small or large living or dead animals together with a small amount of vegetable matter. Dead fish, crayfish, snails, and insects are also acceptable.

Care

- Keep your limbs out of their way.

- Check under your covers before you get into bed, particularly if you own a snake, because they like to cozy up to anything warm.

AMPHIBIANS

Salamanders, caecilians (big wormlike things), frogs, and toads are cold-blooded, with soft, scaleless skin. They represent the early stage of evolution when animals first crawled out of the water to live on land as they developed the ability to breathe air.

Amphibia means "double life" and speaks to the ability of these Creatures of the Black Lagoon— ah, I mean these delightful, charming, and talented amphibians—to exist in water or on land at various stages of their development. Even though they can dwell on land, they still need to be near water so they can keep their eggs moist and complete their larval state.

During their water phase, amphibians, like fish, have gills to help them absorb oxygen from the water. Some will retain their gills and never leave the water permanently. But most will gradually assimilate the gills as they grow out of the larval stage. Their lungs will begin to function and, by the time their metamorphosis is complete, they will be air-breathing land dwellers able to creep, hop, climb, or burrow, similar to human young.

Advantages

- They make great science projects.

- They can play with you equally as well on land and in water. (A serious advantage; this is the only category of pet that can do this and not be tempted to eat you at the same time. Those reptiles like to play rough.)

- You'll never have to worry about someone stealing this pet.

Disadvantages

- They're a little on the slimy side to hold.

- Drivers don't stop for them when they try to cross the road.

- They shrivel up if you forget to keep their swimming pool full.

Housing

- A box with a little moss, a few pebbles, and a small swimming pool is a must.

Food

- Insects, flies, worms . . . things like that.

Care

- Don't pull their arms or legs off to see if they'll grow back.

FISH

Overwhelming in their diversity, fish make up more than half of all vertebrate species. Even though we think of them as having fins, scales, and gills, not all do. What they all have in common is that they live in water and have a supporting structure of either a cartilage rod or a spinal column down their backs.

Fish occupy almost every body of water in the world. Some can be found over large geographic ranges and can tolerate a broad spectrum of conditions, while others are known to inhabit only a single stream or lake, or even just one small desert oasis.

Because they are cold-blooded, their body temperature fluctuates according to the surrounding water. Even though the temperature tolerance of an individual species may be only fifteen to twenty degrees, the total range of all species is from waters of below freezing to those of more than one hundred degrees.

For pet purposes, the most common type of fish are tropical fish. Because of their brilliant and beautiful colors and fluid movements, they are mesmerizing to watch. Of course for those pet owners who won't buy anything unless it has teeth, there is always the piranha.

Advantages

- They are hard to lose. They're always right where you left them.

- There's no telltale bark, chirp, or meow to give away their presence to pet-hating landlords.

- You don't have to get up in the middle of the night to let them out.

- No matter how small your apartment or house is, they'll fit in it.

- If you want to raise guppies for fun and profit, they multiply rapidly and prodigiously, sort of like compound interest.

Disadvantages

- They don't tell good jokes.

- It's hard to give them a proper burial at sea unless you happen to live by the ocean. (Although I've been told that salt added to the commode is an acceptable substitute for landlocked maties.)

Housing

- If you don't have an extra sink or bathtub, an aquarium is recommended. Or if you want extra help staying on your diet, you can use your glass cookie jar. (Fish aren't quite as tempting. And even if you forget and pop a fish, thinking it's a cookie, they're lower in calories.)

Food

- Must be in crumb or microscopic size.

- Symptom of overfeeding: They float belly up. (See disadvantages: burial.)

Care

- Fishes generally don't like to be held.

- It is also important not to throw the fish out with the fish water when it's time to clean the tank.

INSECTS

Of all the creatures in existence, the insect population is the most abundant. Because of their extraordinary numbers and diversity, I won't try to categorize them except to say that they are relatively small in size, multiply rapidly and in large numbers, and are short-lived.

More often than their much larger counterparts, insects can strike fear and terror into the hearts of man. Observe the wide-eyed, frantically swatting, hopping-up-and-down, grimacing victim of the remark "You have a big bug crawling in your hair."

For centuries the Chinese have considered

crickets lucky. They not only keep crickets as pets but have fashioned special tiny cages for them.

Even though we don't readily think of insects as pets, it is unlikely that you will pass through childhood without one. A common rite of hot summer nights is children ecstatically chasing fireflies, trying to collect them in jars with holes punched in the lids so they can have their very own live nightlights. And what about children who spend entire afternoons gathering their caterpillar's favorite leaves so they can watch the wonderous transformation of the caterpillar to the cocoon to the butterfly? And let's not forget the concern of the child who wants to know if all ladybugs are really ladies, and if so, what happened to the gentlemen bugs.

Advantages

- Insects don't cost anything and are in plentiful supply.

- If you decide that it is the wrong pet for you, you don't have to worry about finding it a good home because of its short life span. It will either die before then, or you can simply set it free out your back door with a clear conscience.

- In case of a nuclear war you can be assured your pet insect will survive—even if you don't.

- Housing and food requirements are minimal.

- Insects are particularly hardy and resistant to disease so you won't have any vet bills.

- If you get tired of the buzzing noise of your pet fly, you can use it to catch yourself a pet fish.

Disadvantages

- They multiply quickly and in large numbers, so it is suggested that you keep only male insects. I have that on strong advisement from a mother whose son had a Jiminy Cricket. It got loose in the house and turned out to be a pregnant Jennifer Cricket.

- They won't make it through the wash in your jeans.

- Showing your new two-inch-long pet waterbug to your friends more often than not clears out the room.

Housing

- Homebuilding for insects is inexpensive. Usually a glass container with a few twigs and some grass for decorating will do. If you live with someone who is queasy and doesn't appreciate all God's creatures, you can empty out the matchsticks into the glass container and put your buddy in the match box. Remember to poke holes in the top for air.

Food

- Food is free and can be collected about the yard. Most insects are vegetarians except for the mosquito and black fly, who prefer a liquid diet of the red stuff.

Care

- Mark your insect with fluorescent paint so if it accidentally gets out of its house, you don't confuse it with the wild kind and promptly kill it.

ET CETERAS

The last category of pets comes from the inanimate and imagination species. These have been quite varied and contain some of the most unusual kinds. Since there are too many to mention, such as pet cars, pet boats, pet dreams, and so on, I will limit my discussion to the following: pet aliens, such as E.T. and Alf; pet rocks, for those who can't bear the thought of their beloved dying; pet couch potatoes, for those desiring company in front of the TV; pet dustbunnies, for those who don't like to vacuum.

Advantages

- They don't die.

- You don't have to remember to feed them.

- They won't be a traitor and like someone else in your family more than you.

- You can store them on a shelf or in memory until you feel like playing with them again.

Disadvantages

- They don't die.

- They won't come to greet you at the door when you get home.

- You never know if they're happy to see you or not.

Housing

- Dustbunnies flourish under beds but will tolerate undisturbed corners.

- Closets for E.T.'s.

- The whole house for Alfs.

- At least six feet of couch for your couch potato. (I've never met a couch potato yet who thought the chair it came in had enough room to really stretch out on.)

- Somewhere where you won't stub your toe for your pet rock.

Food

- Dust for dustbunnies.

- Reeses Pieces for E.T.

- Alfs are the least fussy and will eat anything.

- Couch potatoes need at least ten commercials a day.

- Pet rocks like dirt under high pressure.

Care

- They can last only as long as your imagination does.

3

How we're going to get along with our pets according to the heavens

Okay. You've decided what kind of pet you want. Now you just have to figure out if the two of you are really going to be compatible.

There you are, standing (most likely in the pet shop or the pound) face-to-face with what seems like an entire world of precious, cuddly little things. You know they all know what you're there for. Each of them looks up at you beseechingly, as if to say "If you wonderful person don't take me home with you, for better or worse, in sickness and in health till death do us part, who knows what fate I'll meet?"

So how do you choose which one to make your own? Sometimes you get lucky and it's love at first sight. Most times, though, we resort to the old hold-them-in-your-arms try or the see-if-they-lick-your-face-and-wag-their-tail try or the I-can't-make-up-my-mind-but-this-one's-the-cutest try. All of those methods can bring less than satisfactory results after you actually get your pet home.

But there is a secret formula that is nearly fool-proof. It was taught to me by my great-great-aunt, second removed, who was a traveling Gypsy in Albania. It's really very simple. Just get the birth date or, if that's unknown, the birth month of your pet to be. Then look up its sun sign in the pages that follow. You can even check its compatibility with your own sign. That's right! We're talking *pet astrology*. If it's good enough for Nancy Reagan, it's probably safe to assume that it's good enough for your pet.

For a description of what your pet will be like, and for some names that may be particularly appropriate, just look up your pet's birth month or date to find its astrological sign. To see how compatible you and your pet will be, just look under your own sign in the section that follows.

Lest you doubt my great-great-aunt, me, and Mrs. Reagan, I would ask you to consider the following pet signs for yourself.

ARIES

BORN:	March 21 through April 20
SYMBOL:	Ram
RULER:	Mars
ELEMENT:	Fire
KEY WORD:	"I am"

So you've chosen a pet from the first sign of the zodiac. You'll certainly have your hands full. The exuberance and dash of an Aries pet can wear out even the hardiest of souls. Then it will have the audacity to sit there and laugh at you when you can't keep up any longer. Sleep—that's only for sissies. Action is where it's at.

The first thing your Aries pet will want to do when you get it home is check out the premises. Being the little commando that it is, it charges right in and takes over. It wants to know all the strategic places for activity. When it has finished scoping out you and the house, it will be off to see the neighborhood, whether that's the birdcage, fish tank, or the next yard over, to discover any points of interest. It will also want to check out any challenges to its number-one position (at least in its own mind, which is the only mind it considers). Never one to avoid a scrap, your Aries pet may come back from its excursion with a cut or two on its face. Don't be the least bit concerned. You can be sure that your pet absolutely trounced the competition. Any pet stupid enough to take on your Aries won't ever do it again.

Don't misunderstand; Aries pets are not vicious and will not go looking for fights, but, ah, they won't exactly try to avoid them either. They are particularly courageous and will not tolerate what they consider to be an injustice. They are very protective of their owners and make great watch pets. No one will ever hurt you if your Aries pet has anything to say about it. They are fiercely loyal.

Because your Aries is independent and needs lots of activities, it will make its own exercise schedule. Since this is not a pet you can tell what to do, just let it go on its own. When it has finally exhausted itself, it will come back. Of course that may take until next week, but eventually Aries pets do get tired and will return. They always come home to regroup. Even though you'd never get them to admit it, they are very family oriented.

It's been pointed out to me that city dwellers don't have the luxury of letting their pets out by themselves. I have several suggestions for just such a pickle: 1) at least twice a day plan on being whisked through the streets at leash's end as your pet takes its "walk," 2) hire a pet-walking service, 3) erect a race track and obstacle course in your home, or 4) don't get an Aries pet.

You don't need to worry about leaving your pet alone for short periods of time. As long as you are home in time to let it out for its run, you won't have any problems. Otherwise you should devise a way that it can get in and out as it pleases, if you want to come home and find things in one piece. Aries pets have tempers. If this condition is met, it may take your pet a day or two to notice you're gone. Aries are not clinging vines. They are very intelligent and fully capable of amusing themselves.

As far as training goes, Aries pets take to discipline naturally. They catch on quickly and usually have good physical coordination. When the training session is over, your pet will let you know. It will simply cease to cooperate and give you that look that says that's enough for now. And you will obey.

Aries pets can play endlessly with children. Then when the kids are exhausted and ready for a nap, your pet will still have plenty of energy to go for a walk or jog with you. They make great buddies and loyal guardians. As long as your Aries is around, things will never be dull.

Especially Appropriate Names for Your Aries

Thundercat
Little Devil
Lightning
Viva
Sassy
Spark Plug
Arrow
Ramrod
Zorro
Napoleon
Imp

Lickety Split
Can Do
Fire Ball
Zoomer
Numero Uno
Zippity-Do-Da
Rin Tin Tin
Courageous
Outlaw
Primo
Bismarck

Scrappy
Tuff Stuff
Moxie
Fonzy
Spear
Vinny
Alpha
Tabasco
Blaze
Gusto

How You and Your Aries Pet Will Get Along If Your Sign Is:

Aries:

You'll understand your pet's bursts of energy. It'll keep right up with you. The only thing you'll have to watch out for is an occasional bout of competitiveness. You'll get more done together than ten other people. You should like each other fine.

Taurus:

You may find this pet's exuberance a little overwhelming. But it would also inspire you to more activity. Where you are Steady Eddie, your Aries is Speedy Gonzalez. Your temperaments are very different, but sometimes that works out well.

Gemini:

You'll appreciate your pet's quick wit and ready-for-anything outlook. Be careful not to egg each other on, or you could push each other past the point of exhaustion. Remember, tomorrow is another day. You two should be natural friends.

Cancer:

Your Aries pet may be a little too aggressive for you. It may tend to dominate you and be insensitive to your feelings. This is not usually one of the best combinations for compatibility.

Leo:

You will like your Aries' courage and heart. No wimp here. Together you two can set the world on fire. You can cooperate beautifully together. You and your Aries will have a spontaneous affinity for each other.

Virgo:

Because you like things done in an orderly way, you may find your pet's impulsiveness exasperating. You may not understand why it acts first and thinks later. This pet will help to remind you that there are other ways of doing things.

Libra:

Aries is your opposite sign in the zodiac. Where you are charm and diplomacy, your Aries pet is action and bluster. You can help tone down your pet's rashness and make it more balanced. This is either a very good match or a very bad one.

Scorpio:

Your pet's up-frontness may surprise you. You are used to going about things more subtly. You can appreciate your pet's fearlessness and desire to protect you. Though it may not have enough mystery or challenge for you, you could enjoy its energy.

Sagittarius:

You two were meant for each other. You both have an innocent, direct way of looking at things. You'll love to play with each other for hours and find each other endlessly amusing. Even if everyone else thinks you're both nuts, what do they know?

Capricorn:

You may want your Aries pet to be more disciplined, which may touch off a power struggle. This pet doesn't want to be told what to do. If you can't accept that, owning this pet will seem more like a tug of war than a loving companionship.

Aquarius:

You will appreciate each other's zaniness and love of freedom. You'll spend many hours exploring new places, and you'll stimulate each other to do more and be more together. You are likely to be instinctive friends.

Pisces:

If you are looking for a guard pet or a pet to get you out of the house, an Aries will do that. But if you are looking for a simpatico soulmate, other signs would be better. Your natures are very different.

TAURUS

BORN: April 21 through May 20
SYMBOL: Bull
RULER: Venus
ELEMENT: Earth
KEY WORD: "I have"

Your Venusian Taurus is probably pretty easy
to look at. That might even be the first thing that
attracts you to this quiet and sweet-natured pet.
There is also something appealing about its uncom-
plicated, practical outlook. Things are what they
are to a Taurus. If you want it, great; if you don't,
someone else will. It doesn't mind, as long as
sombody feeds it supper.

I do believe the expression "creature comfort"
must have been invented by a Taurus. Your pet will
be looking for a nice place to stay and won't be
happy in anything less than a three-star accommo-
dation. If it is a four-legged pet and it decides it likes
your bed (Taureans like to rest frequently), then
that's where it will preside. Don't even try to dis-
suade it from its chosen spot. You haven't experienced stubborn until you've met up with a Taurus.
It will be easier and less time-consuming to give in,

give your bed to your pet, and go buy yourself another one.

This pet won't be rushing off to see the neighborhood sights right away. First it wants to feel entirely accustomed to you and its new home. Once it has settled into the daily routine, then it will be interested in seeing what the local color has to offer.

Your Taurus pet likes company and seldom will be found alone. It will stay lovingly by your side, or if you are not available, it will find a local playmate. What it won't do is go find a bunch of strangers to hang out with. Taurus pets prefer to spend time with people and other animals they really care about. They may be noticeably choosy about whom they pick for pals out of the available selection. They're not interested in fleeting friendships or superficial infatuations. If they like or love you, it's usually for life. Of course, if they don't like you, that's usually for life, too.

If your pet does bring home a friend from the neighborhood, it will expect you to be a gracious host and feed its buddy a little tidbit also. Once you have taken care of their tummies, they will go off happily and play. A small note of warning: If you have a garden, put a fence around it. One of your pet's favorite play activities is digging holes in anything softer than granite. Taureans love the dirt and often can be found burying themselves or some recently discovered treasure for safekeeping.

Even though your pet may not like to exercise strenuously, it should enjoy a healthy and robust constitution. Taureans are seldom sick. Still, it's not a bad idea to walk, fly, or swim your pet occasionally. Otherwise it tends to get a little portly as it gets older.

Taureans are usually well behaved and can be left alone without putting the fear of God into you about what you'll find when you get home. Just make sure they're comfortable and have enough food and water. They'll wait patiently until you return.

These pets are very trainable and naturally obedient. Plan on spending some time teaching your Taurus pet because it likes to learn slowly and thoroughly. Once your pet does learn something, you can count on it being indelibly etched in its memory.

In general, Taureans make excellent family pets. They are wonderfully trustworthy with children, playing with kids with care and watchfulness. They are tolerant and forgiving of rough behavior. They're also just as happy to sit by Grandma's chair and watch soap operas with her all day.

Especially Appropriate Names for Your Taurus:

Gopher	Molasses	Bon Bon
One Step	Lover	Munchie
Sweets	Snoozer	Paolo
Bear	Digger	Marmaduke
Doe Eyes	Candy	Teobold
Eeyore	Garfield	Stillman
Honey Bun	Bull	Masher
Tank	Elsie	Hannibal
Steady Eddy	Balzac	Moose
Artist	Walker	Tree
Ferdinand	Yogi	

How You and Your Taurus Pet Will Get Along If Your Sign Is:

Aries:

You may find your Taurus pet a tad on the slow side. Actually they're not slow, just methodical. You could learn a lot about pacing yourself by following you pet's lead. Its peaceful nature will either make you feel impatient or soothed.

Taurus:

You'll both enjoy wonderful meals and pleasant walks. Since your pet goes at the same speed, you won't feel pressed for time and can stop to smell the roses. You may react to each other's stubbornness— the pot calling the kettle black.

Gemini:

Your Taurus pet may be too much into the earthly pleasures for your taste. But just knowing it's around can give you a great sense of security. Your pet will hold down the fort while you're off doing twenty things at once.

Cancer:

You will like the stability and calmness of your Taurus pet. Each of you will give the other a sense of nurturing and attentiveness. Since you're both basically homebodies, you have many interests and needs in common. This is a good match.

Leo:

Your Taurus pet likes being the center of attention, as you do. There could be a struggle for the limelight here. You both have very strong wills and ways of doing things. If they happen to be the same, you've got a winner. If not, this is not a favorable pair.

Virgo:

This pet will overwhelm you with affection and care. You should enter into an immediate rapport. You both like to be thorough and practical. You will be tickled pink with a Taurus sidekick.

Libra:

You both fancy the good life because you are both ruled by Venus. Be careful not to encourage the gluttonous side of your pet. It already likes food well enough. Otherwise you should find each other to be gentle and loving.

Scorpio:

This could be a rather explosive combination, for better or worse. You'll either have an intense attraction for your Taurus pet, or find that it reminds you of everything you don't like about yourself. Only you can tell which side a Taurus brings out in you.

Sagittarius:

You might find this pet somewhat sedentary and not as spontaneous as you'd like. You need to give your Taurus pet time to adjust to your flexibility. You can both enjoy the outdoors together. You both like to seek out a good time.

Capricorn:

You two will see eye to eye on pretty much everything. Your Taurus pet desires a pleasant environment, and you'll have the wherewithal to provide that. You both crave security and can give each other a sense of roots.

Aquarius:

According to your cosmic views, a Taurus may seem slightly earthbound. But this pet can help give you a sense of proportion. Don't cringe. I didn't say limitation. If you resist trying to change your pet, you'll have a loyal pal.

Pisces:

You'll like your Taurus pet's easygoing nature. Its tendency toward quiet won't crash in on your sensitive nerves. Your pet will gladly shower you with affection. Feel free to share your dream world with your newfound friend.

GEMINI

BORN: May 21 through June 20
SYMBOL: Twins
RULER: Mercury

ELEMENT: Air
KEY WORD: "I think"

If you would really like two pets but can only afford one, or have room for only one, then a Gemini pet is for you. You get two personalities in the body of one pet. You can even give it two names if you'd like. Something like Jekyll and Hyde would be appropriate, as Geminis give new meaning to the notion of mercurial change.

Your Gemini pet has tons of energy and will certainly keep you in shape. You can count on spending lots of time getting your aerobics in by chasing after it when it tears through your house—bouncing off walls, furniture, and anything else it can use as a jungle gym. If you are really serious about getting yourself on a fitness regimen, put on your running shoes, get yourself in the "on your mark" position by the back door, and call your pet to make its daily duty. When you see a streak of lightning shoot past you, that's your cue to begin the race. Just follow the blur as your pet zooms through the streets, across neighbors' yards, up hills, down alleyways, behind the garbage cans, through newly planted gardens . . . Finally, when you've incurred the wrath of all your neighbors, your pet will bring you back home nonchalantly, smiling innocently at you from the back porch as you come puffing and sweating up the path.

Because of your pet's healthy curiosity and love of change, you can count on being taken on a new route through the neighborhood every day. Of course, don't be so silly as to think that you might actually catch your pet while it's on the loose. Remember, this is intended only to be an exercise in futility.

Gemini pets are great company and are quite social. They love to talk and often make use of their voice box, if they have one. They'll improvise if they don't; these pets need to express themselves. It's also common to find them eavesdropping around a gathering of talking people. They can be quite nosy. They want to know everything that's going on around them. It's that insatiable curiosity again. Expect that, in a matter of days, this pet will be on speaking terms with every person and pet in the neighborhood, a feat that you still haven't accomplished after having lived there for three years.

If you have to leave this pet alone, make sure it has plenty of things to play with. Otherwise you may come home one day to find that your resourceful Gemini got creative while you were out and made a toy out of your favorite stuffed chair, computer, shoe, plant, or anything else remotely accessible. These pets are good at improvising.

You don't need to worry about exercising your pet. On the contrary, you'll be trying to find ways to keep it quiet, or at least relatively calm. This is a pet that you might like to keep outside most of the time.

You should find your pet remarkably easy to train; if you have a talking parrot, for instance, it will teach itself to talk. Gemini pets actually like learning new tricks and will delight in entertaining you. Start off with short training sessions because they easily become restless and bored. It's best to begin training inside, since the outdoors offers too many tempting distractions.

These pets will calm down a little as they grow into adulthood, but they'll always have a youthful, playful quality. This is wonderful if you buy a Gemini pet for your child to grow up with, though not such a good idea if you are a septuagenarian looking for a pet who will stay quietly by your side.

If you have boundless energy and enthusiasm, are young at heart, hate being alone, and like someone to play with at a moment's notice, then a Gemini pet could be your perfect match.

Especially Appropriate Names for Your Gemini

Short Stop	Zig Zag	Skittles
Jabber	Early Bird	Kanga
Scamp	Dennis the	Munchkin
Curious	Menace	Calypso
June Bug	Ad Lib	Quicksilver
Nosy	Youngster	Penny
Chatter Box	Road Runner	Niccolo
Squirt	Racer	Elissa
Mad Hatter	Freckles	Be Bop
Wiggles	Bubbly	Jimini
Yakker	Echo	Gabby

How You and Your Gemini Pet Will Get Along If Your Sign Is:

Aries:

You'll appreciate each other's love of activity. You won't have any problem with your pet's manic energy and desire to get into everything. You'll think that's normal. That's why a Gemini pet is perfect for you.

Taurus:

You may find your pet's coquettishness cute. It loves to entertain, and you make an appreciative audience. Since you have the stronger will, you shouldn't have any problems helping your pet channel its enthusiasm.

Gemini:

This match is like having two owners and two pets, as Gemini is the sign of the twins. Double the pleasure, double the fun. You certainly won't feel at a loss for company. On the contrary, you'll feel stimulated twenty-five hours a day.

Cancer:

The Gemini pet may not fill enough of your need for having an affectionate companion. Not a homebody, it will be busy running off here and there. Even though you may find it delightful, you might prefer a more placid pet.

Leo:

You'll like this vivacious pet. It will keep you hopping. Your pet will happily include you in all its activities. Take it for a walk and watch all the people your pet will introduce you to. This pet will be great for your social life.

Virgo:

You might feel annoyed by your pet's tendency to start off in a million directions at the same time, as you like to finish what you start before moving on. You will appreciate its quick mind and its physical agility.

Libra:

You'll like your pet's social skills and mental graces.
You share very harmonious personalities. You have
compatible ideas on what makes a good relationship
and will fill each other's needs without making a big
thing out of it.

Scorpio:

A Gemini pet could appear slightly superficial or
fickle for your intense needs. You may find its love
of busyness distracting. If you think this pet is hard
to figure out, you're overlooking the obvious. What
you see is what you get.

Sagittarius:

Here's your opposite in the zodiac. You both love to
explore. But a Gemini's exploration is more of the
mind while yours is more in the doing. You may find
your pet all talk and no action. Or you two could
take off on a happy journey with no end.

Capricorn:

You may not know what to make of this bundle of
nerves. You'll think that if you could harness all
that energy you could start your own power plant.
Others have tried and failed. If you can't enjoy this
pet's diversity, pass it over for another.

Aquarius:

You'll think your Gemini pet is as bright as a new
penny. You won't have any problem with its electric
personality. Because you are not possessive, you'll
welcome all the friends your pet brings over. The
more, the merrier.

Pisces:

The Gemini pet may short-circuit your sensibilities. You need time to work into new situations, while your pet jumps first and looks on the way down. There are basic temperamental differences between you.

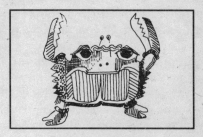

CANCER

BORN: June 21 through July 21
SYMBOL: Crab
RULER: Moon
ELEMENT: Water
KEY WORD: "I feel"

Make sure your Cancer pet has had enough time to be weaned from its mommy before you get it. Nurturing and being nurtured are very important to this pet. Cancers are sensitive enough as it is without traumatizing them by taking them away from home and family too soon.

When you do manage to get your Cancer bundle home, don't be surprised if you can't find it for a day or two. Cancer pets are quite shy and may not acclimate immediately. Just leave food out where your pet can find it, and it will come out at night to

eat while everyone is asleep. If your pet is missing
for too long, check your closets, under the beds, behind the couch—anywhere you would think to hide
if you were looking for a safe haven in an unknown
world. Lo and behold, there it will be, all a-quiver
and so fragile looking. You won't be able to resist
scooping up this bedraggled babe into your arms
while you tenderly coo little nothings and rock it
gently back and forth. Of course, if it's a fish or an
elephant we're talking about, simply cooing to it
will suffice. I guarantee that this pet will bring out
the mother instinct in you.

A healthy dose of affection is needed bring your
Cancer pet out of its shell. Once your pet has
adopted you as its very own, you won't find a more
loyal, devoted, and protective pal. It is quite common for Cancers to get attached to a favorite family
member and become a one-person pet. They seem to
feel more secure when they have only one person to
focus on and can get upset if there are too many
people around or too much commotion.

If you want your pet to go outside and get some
exercise or sun, you won't have to worry about it
straying off. Cancers are homebodies and aren't
likely to embark on any expeditions. If they are co-
erced away by some other neighborhood pet, they'll
probably return on their own in a few hours. They
don't like to eat in strange places and prefer to sleep
in their own beds at night. If your pet isn't back by
bedtime, maybe you should go looking for it, as it
could be lost or unwillingly detained somewhere
and in need of your help.

Your Cancer pet will behave quite nicely when
left alone for short periods of time, and will happily

and enthusiastically greet you at the door when you come back. These pets don't do as well if they are left for an extended period of time. They can become quite despondent and inconsolable. Cancers can hold grudges longer than almost any other pet. They don't forget. So if you have to be away for long, bring them home an extra-special treat and plan on giving them your undivided attention for the rest of that day. At the very least, let them follow you around from room to room and lie on your feet to make sure you aren't going to be taking off again anytime soon.

These pets are usually pretty easy to train. But you must be gentle with them. Don't yell at them or hit them. Cancer pets are very emotional and easily crushed. You can undo all your good work in an instant and find yourself back at square one. Patience and kindness are the keys to success with your sensitive Cancer.

Because of their watchfulness and protectiveness, Cancer pets are good with children. As they get older, they tend toward inactivity and prefer a retiring environment. Thus they are also wonderful pets for older owners and will be happy to sit with you on the porch as you both watch the evening sunsets.

Especially Appropriate Names for Your Cancer

Tenderfoot	Muffin	Bambi
Pooh	Cuddles	Snuggles
Moon Beam	Tides	Underfoot
Lamb Chop	Hermit	Fluster
Nanny	Possum	Sidestep

Shy Baby	Noah	Suds
Moody	Cook	Linus
Watchful	Puddles	Urchin
Pearl	Spumoni	Muffy
Thoreau	Buttermilk	Sweet Pea
Bashful	Henny Penny	

How You and Your Cancer Pet Will Get Along If Your Sign Is:

Aries:

You may think your Cancer pet needs too much re-assurance or care for your independent ways. Your impatience could crush this pet. However, if you are looking for a stay-at-home pet to be there only for you, this combination might work out.

Taurus:

This pet is exactly what you need to feel cared for and loved. It will look after you cheerily and stay by your side warmly. You'll share a true affinity with your nurturing companion. Some say this is a match made in heaven.

Gemini:

Your Cancer pet can have a stabilizing effect on you and act as a reminder to come home every now and again. You may not understand its reclusive tendencies, but not everyone needs as much stimulation as you do.

Cancer:

You two might never go out of the house and think that's wonderful. You'll both share a love for home and family that is awe-inspiring. Your pet will instinctively respond to your feelings. Sometimes this can be too much of a good thing.

Leo:

This pet will make you feel like the king or queen you think you are. Your humble servant will indulge you with nonstop affection and tenderness. Remember to praise this pet and not take it for granted because its feelings get hurt very easily.

Virgo:

You'll like the idea of a pet being there to pamper you after a long hard day. You'll appreciate your Cancer's gentle ways. It will stay quiet when you need to think and enthusiastically go along to play when you want to play.

Libra:

You might find this pet to be a little overemotional. Actually it could just be that it's responding to your flair for the dramatic and becomes melodramatic in its attempt to be like you. This may be a tiring combination.

Scorpio:

You'll love the emotional sensitivity of this pet. Finally, a pet who can match your sense of intrigue and intensity! Your Cancer pet will loyally watch over you, making you feel safe and secure. You can be real soulmates.

Sagittarius:

This pet could be somewhat timid for your adventurous spirit. Its tendency toward seriousness may

dampen your boisterous sense of humor. But then
again, sometimes what you think is funny really
isn't. A Cancer pet is a good test for that.

Capricorn:

Cancer is your opposite sign. You may fluctuate between enjoying your pet's need to be taken care of
and to take care of you, and feeling trapped by the
responsibility. Your need is to conquer the world,
while your pet's need is to be loved.

Aquarius:

You may be a little flustered by your pet's depen-
dency on you for its well-being. You could feel
smothered by its need for your attention. If you
don't overreact, you might find that you like its nurturing, affectionate ways.

Pisces:

Two gentle souls floating on a sea of peace. You'll
seem to be able to read each other's minds. You'll
protect each other from the unpleasantness of life,
while ensuring each other's well-being. You'll spend
many happy years together.

LEO

BORN: July 22 through August 22
SYMBOL: Lion
RULER: Sun
ELEMENT: Fire
KEY WORD: "I will"

You can always tell Leo pets in the pet store; they're the ones showing off, trying to get your attention. They think they are wonderful, and they expect you to think the same. Of course they are the ones you want to take home. How could you even consider anyone else? Or so your Leo will expect you to realize—if you are worthy of owning it. One thing Leos are not, you'll quickly learn, is humble or shy.

Leo pets will rule your roost with dignity and pride—most of the time. (They've been known to be incredibly childish and undignified when they are particularly happy or have a friend over to play with.) They are very territorial and assume that they should have the run of the place without question. While they are usually good watch pets, it won't necessarily be to protect you. They just don't like to share their domain if they think there will

be competition for your affection. If they do sense
that you actually are in danger, they will come ag-
gressively to your rescue. Nobody messes with a
Leo's possession (which you are) and gets away with
it. Which brings me to another point. You will have
to redefine your concept of who the pet is here. Because, according to your Leo, all things were put on
this earth to entertain it, including you.

A Leo pet requires lots of exercise and good
food. It wants to keep in tiptop shape so that when
it struts its stuff, you can fully appreciate its beauty
and form. Leos demand to be looked at and insist on
affection, love, and praise. You can never overcom-
pliment your Leo. And if you don't give it the attention it needs—excuse me, I mean deserves—don't be
surprised if it looks elsewhere. There are plenty of
other pets and people in the world who will recog-
nize your king or queen. There's nothing more in-
dignant than an ignored Leo.

Also, don't get a Leo pet if you don't want all
the other animals in the neighborhood over on occa-
sion. It's an old tradition that Leos like to hold
court. Actually, they are extremely friendly and
love playmates. And if there is going to be a leader
of the pack, guess whose pet it is going to be? They
like to have fun, fun, fun. They have no concept of
too much of a good thing and are avid practitioners
of the adage "If a little bit is good, a lot must be
better."

This bring us to the disciplining and training of
your little darling. Forget it! Actually, it's not all
that hopeless. Leos are very intelligent and are capable of learning any feat (that is, if you can get
them to take you seriously). Work is not in their

vocabulary, so unless you plan to make an enjoyable game out of it, you might as well give up. Sometimes bribes do work. The promise of a select table scrap or a bright new bauble has been known to induce temporary interest and attention.

If you have to leave your Leo pet alone, you should check on its mood first to determine what course of action to take. If your Leo is in a good mood, you're pretty safe to leave it inside. But if you detect the least bit of a snit brewing, outdoors is the only reasonable choice if you value your possessions. This pet does have a temper.

Since Leos are always children at heart, they are great companions for kids. As they mature—let me rephrase that—as they grow older, they just get to be bigger kids. But they are so lovable and loyal and, in many ways, so innocent that they can't help but keep you young at heart too, no matter what your age. They always bring a ray of sunshine to those who have the good sense to love them.

Especially Appropriate Names for Your Leo

King Pin	Gusto	Shiner
Big Deal	Strutter	Whoopi
Queenie	Peter Pan	Hart
Razzmatazz	Good Time	Uppity
Full of It	Charlie	Felicity
Caesar	Jazz	Tux
Sunshine	Peacock	Top Kat
Ego	Bold Strokes	Rex
Little Lion	Your Highness	High Fi
Lancelot	Rajah	Adonis
Romeo	Goldie	Victoria

How You and Your Leo Pet Will Get Along If Your Sign Is:

Aries:

Your Leo pet's bravado will entertain you indefinitely. You both lean toward action and will keep each other stimulated. What you won't do is sit around the house staring pie-eyed at each other. Too much to do and see together for that kind of mush.

Taurus:

The lion roars, the bull bellows, and they're both stubborn. The extravagant lion may do things in a way that threatens your sense of security. If you can manage to get along with each other, you won't find a more loyal pet.

Gemini:

You'll get a kick out of your pet's flash and dash. You'll both enjoy having lots of company; you—so you can show off your mind; your Leo—so it can show off itself. This is an irrepressible combination.

Cancer:

A Leo pet will help bring you out of your shell. It will pick you up when your spirits are low and teach you how to soar when your spirits are high. This pet will also shine under your lavish attention.

Leo:

You'll either think you're both God's gift to the planet, or you'll drive each other nuts as you elbow for the center stage. At the very least, you'll understand your pet's attention-seeking behavior.

Virgo:

You may find it hard to believe that anyone can be that theatrical because you are usually so demure. That may be part of the fascination you'll have for this pet. If a little of that could only rub off on you, there's nothing you couldn't do.

Libra:

You'll like the regal way your pet carries itself. This pet will captivate you with its style and vitality. People will comment on what a striking pair you make. But all of that is small potatoes compared to the love you'll have for each other.

Scorpio:

You may be attracted and annoyed at the same time by your pet's abundant life force. Where you are contained, your Leo is expansive. You may try to overdiscipline your pet to mold it into being more like you. This is a high-voltage combination.

Sagittarius:

Your pet couldn't find a better audience for its antics. You two will spend most of your time clowning around. This is the party duo par excellence. You'll encourage each other to bring out your best. This is a happy match.

Capricorn:

A Leo pet may be more flamboyant than you'd like. In your own quiet way, you are usually the center of attention and may not approve of a pet who so shamelessly seeks the same. Secretly you could be envious of the sun that shines automatically on your Leo.

Aquarius:

It may be a new experience for you to have a more self-centered pet when you are so other-people centered. Because a Leo is your opposite, it can show you what you lack and that is to put yourself first once in a while.

Pisces:

You'll appreciate your pet's gift for the dramatic because you have such a vivid imagination yourself. You can also learn a lot from your Leo's innate self-confidence. This pet may not always be sensitive to your moods.

VIRGO

BORN: August 23 through September 22
SYMBOL: Virgin
RULER: Mercury
ELEMENT: Earth
KEY WORD: "I analyze"

While there are certainly more flamboyant and boisterous pets you could choose over a Virgo, you'd be hard-pressed to find one who is more loyal and willing to serve you. Your Virgo just seems to know when you need to be cheered up or taken care of, and will set about doing so quietly and calmly. If you've had a bad day at the office, you can count on your pet to meet you at the door with slippers and newspaper.

But don't be fooled by your helper's appearance of not having any needs of its own other than tending to yours. Virgos have very specific needs—one of which is living in clean and neat surroundings. This pet can't function in chaos or messes. Virgos are decidedly fastidious and will seem nervous and anxious in anything less than an orderly environment. That's not to say that there isn't the occasional odd slob among them. But it's rare.

The other thing your Virgo pet will appreciate is lots of stimulation. Virgos like company, but only if there is some purpose to the gathering. They like things to be structured and need to feel secure about their position in the home. Because they respond to a work ethic, they might be a plowhorse, a seeing-eye dog, a favorite milk cow, or the like. They are not used to having fun just for the sake of having fun. Virgo pets don't know the meaning of the word lazy. More often than not, it's because they are too busy striving for some idea of perfection or service. With gentle coaxing, you can teach them to relax.

Your pet will be putty in your hands if you occasionally take the time to bathe, brush, and groom it. It always feels better when it's nice and clean. Then, if you don't need it for any pressing task, it will dutifully go off to play.

Virgos are not overly aggressive and are seldom found at the center of a ruckus. As a matter of fact, if you do find it near the dust cloud, it's likely to be the one trying to break the matter up. They prefer to avoid scenes. They are easy to get along with and usually well liked by other animals and people.

It follows that your pet is also very easy to leave alone. You won't find torn papers or ripped furniture on your return. Everything will be exactly as you've left it. Maybe even a little tidier. And still your pet will be there waiting with slippers for you to appear. Feel free to tell it your troubles of the day too. Virgos are good listeners and very understanding.

No need to develop an exercise program for your Virgo. It is very conscientious about health and fitness, almost overly so. And it would appreciate it if you would feed it a balanced diet. This pet wants to take care of itself so it can stay active in old age.

Your pet will look forward to being trained. It likes to do things it can get better at. Virgos are very versatile and agile, and can perform almost any trick or feat you can think up. The more complicated, the better. Unknown to most people, Virgos are also the class clowns and will have fun outdoing you in creating their own tricks, since they'll find yours way too simple and unimaginative.

These gentle souls make good companions for anyone. They are cautious with children and like to make themselves useful to adults. They will serve you long and well until they are no longer able. These pets will make it all too easy for you to take them for granted, so remember to take good care of them too.

Especially Appropriate Names for Your Virgo

Prudence
Higgins
Woodchip
Careful
Messenger
Hypochondriac
Pythagoras
Clown
Jigsaw
My Man
  Godfrey
Patience

Computer
Pickpocket
Tutor
Doc
Fretful
Morris
Ceres
Fussbudget
Grandma
  Moses
Willy

Stitches
Cactus
Patches
Joggaty
That's Enough
Broomtail
Q-tip
Chastity
Crispin
Prentice
Virtue

How You and Your Virgo Pet Will Get Along If Your Sign Is:

Aries:

You'll be impressed with your pet's thoroughness even if it is somewhat alien to your nature. Your Virgo pet can finish what you start. But basically you operate at very different speeds and styles.

Taurus:

You'll like to do things outdoors together and you'll share many interests. Like you, your pet is very practical, so it's unlikely you'll have any emotional misunderstandings. You have exceptionally compatible natures and should get along beautifully.

Gemini:

Your pet may have a hard time getting used to your
scattered nature. You may see your Virgo pet as
overly cautious. Be careful not to try to get it to do
too many things at once. Not everyone is
ambidexterous, as you are.

Cancer:

You will love your Virgo's attention and sensitivity
to the little nuances of your moods. Your pet will
appreciate the special care you give it. You both
have your own systems of looking after the needs of
the other.

Leo:

Your pet will be happy to wait on you hand and foot.
It has no desire to steal the show. Be careful not to
abuse a good thing, though. Your Virgo hates being
taken for granted. So remember to give as well as
take.

Virgo:

While you go brush your teeth after a meal, your
counterpart can lick the crumbs up from the floor.
Then everything will be as neat and tidy as you
both like. So what if others think you're compulsive-
obsessive about cleanliness? Your pet understands.

Libra:

You'll like how careful your pet is with your nice
things. Its gentle nature and quiet ways will fit
right in with your lifestyle. You'll appreciate your
Virgo pet's innate intelligence and be charmed by
its watchfulness for your welfare.

Scorpio:

Your Virgo pet is earthy and can share your lust for life. You can bring out the mischievous side of each other in a fun way. Your pet will faithfully tend to your needs and allow for the depths and heights of your moods without a second thought.

Sagittarius:

You may feel your pet is too picky about not having its routine disturbed. Your Virgo pet may not be ready at less than a moment's notice to take off for parts unknown. Now, if you're willing to give it at least two minutes, you'll have no problem.

Capricorn:

Your pet's orderliness and common sense will appeal to you. There will be no upsetting melodramatics or tantrums. This pet will be happy to stay sedately by your side. You'll have a deep and lasting bond and a worthy friend.

Aquarius:

Your Virgo pet may help keep you attached to this world. Its practical, predictable routines can serve to remind you what day it is. Though you are structurally different in your view of reality, you can appreciate your pet's objective outlook.

Pisces:

You may find this pet too unemotional in its response to things. Actually, your Virgo pet is quite sensitive in a reserved way. As this pet is your zodiac opposite, you'll either feel an instinctive connection to it, or not care for it at all.

LIBRA

BORN: September 23 through October 22
SYMBOL: Scales of Justice
RULER: Venus
ELEMENT: Air
KEY WORD: "I balance"

Ah, the beauty and charm of a Libra pet has seduced many a pet buyer. Their refined and graceful carriage can make even the largest among them seem as if they float on air. They possess an inherent elegance and presence, which makes them naturals if you are looking for a show pet. But don't be fooled by the saying that beauty is only skin deep. Your Libra pet also has a sweet-natured temperament, which makes it a very pleasant companion. Looks and likability—an unbeatable combination.

If you are a stickler for the good things in life, and follow that up by having the best of everything in your home, Libras will fit right in. They are also great appreciators of aristocratic living. They will move daintily around your expensive antiques and appreciate your state-of-the-art sound system. They do best in a pleasant and peaceful environment.

Which also goes without saying: If you are looking for a pet you can have a raucous, rough-house good time with, you might want to bypass these more ethereal spirits. They can seem high-strung or nervous in an overstimulating environment.

For as much as your Libra pet enjoys the finer things, don't be surprised if it brings home a less than well-kempt neighborhood down-and-outer. While Librans can be entirely snobbish about material possessions, they are unusually fair and broad-minded in their associations. Remember, their symbol is the scale of justice. They find friends equally as well in low and high places. Everyone has worth to them. Since they like to socialize, they are never at a loss for buddies, because anyone will do.

Since Librans do prefer company, they don't always do well when they're left alone. Not that they'll tear into your Louis XIV couch or anything like that. Physical revenge is seldom their style. They are far too well mannered and subtle for such a base display of temper. Instead they may indulge in some unconstrained moping. Don't underestimate what an effective form of punishment this can be. Be prepared to do some serious cajoling when you get home. One pet owner has confessed to me that he found his pet's mood so disconcerting that he went out and bought another pet (not a Libra) to keep his Libra happy. Did I also mention that Librans can be world-class actors?

Because your pet may be a trifle vain, you don't have to worry about making sure it exercises. Even though its motive may not be its love for athletic activity, it will demurely trot or fly around the block to ensure that nothing sags or goes soft before its time. You can easily pick up your Libran's spirit by having a little treat waiting for it on its return. This sign, perhaps more than any other, appreciates being pampered.

As for training, your pet will endure your instructions politely. Librans are very good at cooperating and should be exceedingly easy to educate. They may seem bored as you put them through their paces. It's not that they don't want to please you—they most certainly do. It's just that they came out of the womb already trained and find it all a little redundant. But if it will make you happy, they'll gladly jump through that hoop one more time.

These pets are affectionate with children and devoted to an older master. They are active enough to be playful but not so hyperactive that you need to keep them outside. Because equality comes so naturally to Librans, they will remember to love everyone in your family, so no one feels left out. It's hard to imagine someone who wouldn't enjoy having a Libra pet for his or her very own.

Especially Appropriate Names for Your Libra

Cutie	Flower	Petunia
Fair Play	Prince	Maybe
Jewel	Beauty	Beau
Pretty Boy	Judge	Lisette
Princess	Lacey	Turtledove
Balance Beam	My Fair Lady	Romeo
Posh	Prince	Willow
Lovey	Charming	Liberty
Lady Grace	Harmony	Cupid
Blythe	Aphrodite	Fluffy
Partner	Chenille	Colin

How You and Your Libra Pet Will Get Along If Your Sign Is:

Aries:

A Libra is the opposite astrological sign from you. This pet can act as a mirror to help show you how others see you. If you are agitated or impatient, your pet will wither. If you show a gentle side, which you do have, your pet will bloom.

Taurus:

You'll think your Libra pet's good taste and good looks are a perfect match for your hedonistic tendencies. You may find this pet overly dainty at times, but not enough to jar your sensibilities. All in all, this is a genial pairing.

Gemini:

Your Libra pet will prove to be a first-class listener for your need to talk. This pet will be a perfect lady or gentleman to all your guests. You won't need any "Beware of Pet" signs to forewarn the unexpected visitors you frequently receive.

Cancer:

You may feel your Libra pet isn't responsive enough to your feelings. Librans have a certain decorum about emotional displays. They might even appear almost judgmental to you at times. But you both desire a peaceful and calm home environment.

Leo:

You should find this pet a splendid match for you. Its elegant poise and gracious personality will reflect well on you. Your Libra will be proud of all the things you do. In your pet's own quiet way, it will keep you feeling well loved.

Virgo:

Your Libra pet will fit right in your nice, neat home. This pet is seldom messy. And it will appreciate all the grooming you give it to keep up its appearance. Since Librans are not pushy, this pet won't get in the way of how you like to do things.

Libra:

A Libra pet with a Libra owner is like the proverbial two peas in a pod. Since Libra is the sign of balance, it's unlikely you'll ever disagree on anything. You both value harmony more than almost anything. You will find each other pleasant and attractive.

Scorpio:

You may think your Libra's please-all policy makes it an unsubstantial pet, as you prefer standing your ground. Yet this pet could help smooth over some of your more brazen tendencies. It is capable of being a calming agent for you.

Sagittarius:

You'll like your Libra pet's lighthearted approach to life. Remember to be affectionate with this pet occasionally, and you'll have a buddy for life. It will also make a good audience for all your antics.

Capricorn:

You may feel this pet is too concerned with keeping up its appearances for your earthy tastes. You'd prefer that it spend all that energy making you the center of its attention. If you remember not to be overly stern, it would be happy to do so.

Aquarius:

Your Libra pal is far too polite to ever wonder about some of your penchants for the unusual. It will go along happily with all your ideas and activities. This pet makes a natural friend and a loving companion for you.

Pisces:

It may take a little time to get a Libra pet to share your wavelength. Your Libra may want to be off visiting the neighbors when you want it to sit quietly with you and share pleasant dreams.

SCORPIO

BORN: October 23 through November 21
SYMBOL: Scorpion
RULER: Pluto
ELEMENT: Water
KEY WORD: "I desire"

Your Scorpio pet may be the one to find you. I've known several who have appeared on their owners' doorsteps in the middle of the night, out of nowhere, to become a permanent part of the family. You can try shooing them away if you want, but it would be a waste of good breath. Once a Scorpio makes up its mind, that's that. You should feel flattered that you were the one to be singled out. Even if you get your pet through more conventional means, there will still be something slightly mysterious about it. Scorpios have an unfathomable quality that makes them seem like pets with a past, or keepers of some hidden secret. Lunacy, you say? You have just revealed that you've never had a Scorpio pet. Scorpio owners will all solemnly nod their heads in agreement as to the inscrutable nature of their pets.

This pet is its own ruler. It's not one to sit around and wait for anything. This is both good and not so good. These pets don't need to be entertained and need only a minimal amount of care. They are very resourceful and self-sufficient. That's the good news. If, for example, you own a Scorpio Husky and there is a chicken coop within a radius of twenty miles and you forget to feed it, you could be in serious trouble. Expect occasional visits from a very unhappy farmer carrying several dead hens in tow. That's the bad news. These pets are instinctive hunters in the most primal sense. They can't help themselves. Forget whatever else you like but don't forget to feed them.

Don't count on quickly housebreaking your pet. Your Scorpio pet has a wild streak that you might be able to contain but that you'll never really tame. These pets are just as happy outdoors as indoors. Actually, they prefer to be outside so they can watch the house and protect it and you from any intruders. They are at once extremely loyal and jealously possessive. They make some of the best watch pets. Nothing gets past their penetrating gaze.

If you must leave your pet home alone, do so at your own risk. It's not that it can't be perfectly well behaved and an absolute angel. But if it's mad at you, it's fully capable of being spiteful. Also, don't leave it alone with a smaller pet unless you leave plenty of food for both. These pets don't require lots of company. This is one of the few signs of the zodiac that actually likes being alone.

Periodic absences are one of the telltale signs of a Scorpio pet. It might only have been off playing with the pet down the street, but it will do so away from prying eyes. No one will see or know its whereabouts until it decides to return. Your Scorpio is also quite amorous and may become known as something as a Casanova in the neighborhood. Ask it if it cares. It doesn't. Reputation means nothing to this passionate pet.

Scorpios don't take well to being told what to do, so don't plan on training your pet quickly and thoroughly. You have to be persistent. Don't be fooled by its irascible nature—Scorpios are usually extremely intelligent but often just as stubborn. If they see that it is important to you, they will give in and cooperate. Once they learn, they never forget.

Also, there is no need to be concerned about Scorpio pets getting enough exercise. They are very active critters. Scorpios regenerate more energy in rest than most other pets use in activity.

If it seems like Scorpio pets are a handful, they

can be. Hopefully that won't scare you off. They can
be very exasperating the first year of their lives because they are so much their own creatures. But
that's exactly what makes them so interesting—
they are always full of surprises. The adage "Age
brings wisdom" is very true for your Scorpio. They
mellow wonderfully with age and have all the best
qualities that people want to have in a pet.

Especially Appropriate Names for Your Scorpio

Dragon Slayer	Midnight	Garbo
Saucy	Eagle Eye	Probe
Pluto	Naughty	Hercules
Intrepid	Stinger	Madam
Brigitte Bar- dog	Tempest	J.R.
Dynamite	Wolf	Sphinx
Panther	Vigilant	Pirate
Shadow	Hawk	Lola
Fearless	Inspector	Scout
Biter of Enemies	Phoenix	Sherlock
	Dostoevski	Desiree

How You and Your Scorpio Pet Will Get Along If Your Sign Is:

Aries:

Here's one pet that not only will be able to keep up
with you, but possibly even outdo you. Yes, I know
it's shocking. But then with a Scorpio pet you'll
have to reevaluate many of your basic premises.
This is a feisty combination.

Taurus:

Your opposite of the zodiac can either stir you on to feats you didn't know you were capable of, or drive you nuts. There's not going to be too much middle ground with this pet. If you don't kill each other the first week, that's a good sign.

Gemini:

The Scorpio pet could show you a thing or two about depth and concentration. Its capacity for feeling will surprise you. You may not quite know what to do with such a live wire. But that's okay, because your Scorpio can manage itself.

Cancer:

Here's an instinctively compatible pairing. Your pet will respond to your nurturing and caring with a deep loyalty and protectiveness. You two just seem to understand each other. This is often an inseparable bond.

Leo:

Anyone for some fireworks? This is sort of like oil and water; they stay more blended when things keep getting shaken up. What you won't have is a dull routine. But then you both find that dramatically intense displays tend to keep things interesting.

Virgo:

An impassioned Scorpio pet is just what you need to put a little spark under you. You can borrow some of its boundless energy and feel inspired to do more.

You will bring out the most positive traits in each other.

Libra:

Initially you may feel overwhelmed by the deep emotional needs of your pet. But once you get used to its all-encompassing moods, you'll find yourself enjoying its attention and love. You won't find a more loyal watch pet.

Scorpio:

This could produce spontaneous combustion or love at first sight. Earthquakes have calmer mannerisms. Most likely you'll like and understand each other. But count on needing to spend lots of time away from each other.

Sagittarius:

Don't laugh at your Scorpio pet's moodiness. Your pet will be even more wounded by your insensitivity to whatever plight it is experiencing. If you can't take this pet seriously, then you are better off not taking it at all.

Capricorn:

You are both believers in playing things close to the chest. You also share deep reserves of talent and regeneration, but your Scorpio pet is more emotionally demonstrative than you. On the whole, this is a complementary match.

Aquarius:

You may not know what to make of this pet. Your emotional temperaments are significantly different.

Where you think everyone belongs to the world, your Scorpio pet thinks you should belong solely to each other.

Pisces:

A Scorpio pet makes a wonderful companion for you. It will look after you protectively when it sees you drifting off into your dream world. It will enthusiastically romp with you when you feel like playing. It will love you forever.

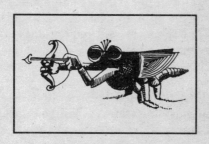

SAGITTARIUS

BORN: November 22 through December 21
SYMBOL: Archer
RULER: Jupiter
ELEMENT: Fire
KEY WORD: "I see"

A Sagittarian pet is one of the most happy-go-lucky creatures you'll ever bump into—literally. While these pets have some of the best dispositions going, they can be somewhat klutzy. They are too busy being excited and interested to pay attention to what their bodies are doing. If you can get them attached to their bodies, they make superb athletes. Whatever these pets do, they do in a big way.

When you get your pet home, it will enthusiastically greet everyone in the family. No shy wallflower here. After it feels that it has had sufficient time to get to know each member of its new family, it will want to explore its new home and neighborhood. And I do mean explore. These pets are natural adventurers and can have a tendency to roam far and wide. You are definitely going to want to get a collar tag or halter with its name and your home phone number on it so when it arrives in Kalamazoo, someone there can call you to come get it. Sagittarians seem to have a sense of direction only in heading out, not in coming home. Maybe because there always seems to be something even more intriguing just around the corner that keeps them looking and moving forward. Unlike Cancers, wherever Sagittarians are around bedtime is home for the night.

Your little wanderer will also make friends from near and far. It likes to travel with the international set. It may even pick up a foreign language or two from FiFi the French poodle or Pedro the Peruvian parrot. These pets don't know the meaning of prejudice. As a matter of fact, the more different they find you, the more interest they'll have in you. It's just one big happy world, and don't try to tell them any different. Expect to have a revolving door of visitors of all shapes, sizes, and species as long as you own your pet.

This is one pet you might want to keep inside when you are not home unless you have some sort of contraption you can tie it to outside. It's not that Sagittarians like being inside so much; they don't. I'm just trying to suggest ways to keep your life simple so you don't have to hire an animal tracker to find out where your pet has gone while you were away. Of course, once you get your Sagittarian trained to stay on your property, it's still a good idea to keep it tied. If it gets bored, it will think nothing of going off to look for you or to find someone else to play with. It might come back on its own, and then again, it might not.

You have to have a sense of humor if you want to train your Sagittarius pet successfully. It loves to goof around and make fun of you. Don't get offended. It will also be the first to make fun of itself. It simply finds everything funny. If you won't let it have a good time, it won't try. Don't waste your time trying to dampen its exuberant spirit. It's much easier to let its zest for living rub off on you. True, you may not get much accomplished in any one training session, but you'll still feel great at the end of it anyway. And eventually Sagittarians do learn.

Since your pet's exercise needs are great, it's ideal if you have a lot of space for it to run around on. If not, you might want to buy it a treadmill or something. Otherwise it will drive you nuts as it does laps around your dining-room table or skids across the living-room floor on your Oriental rug, smashing into the coffee table as it envisions itself scoring a home run. Oh yes, that's another one of it's irrepressible traits: It has an incredible imagination.

If your life is devoid of any regular joy or you

have forgotten how to laugh, you need this pet. It
will keep you looking at the world in a fresh way.
Whether you are a child or an adult, you'll never
find a better pal.

Especially Appropriate Names for Your Sagittarius:

Hobo	Funny Face	Puck
Skywalker	Sport	Mr. Ed
Wack-a-do	Chuckles	Father
Zany	Rover	O'Grady
Happy	Goofy	Tally Ho
Merry Weather	Traveler	Tinkerbell
Snoopy	Benji	Ranger
Lucky	Clown	Quest
Joker	Bedouin	Dasher
Reckless	Ulysses	Scooter
Gypsy	Huckleberry	Jupiter

How You and Your Sagittarius Pet Will Get Along If Your Sign Is:

Aries:

You'll like your Sagittarius pet's joy for life and
sense of humor. Plus, your pet has an abundance of
energy, like you, and will have no problem keeping
up with you. This is usually a pretty successful combination.

Taurus:

You may find that this pet enjoys a little more of the
ruckus of life than your quiet temperament likes.
But if there are other playmates around, your pet
will be happy. You'll enjoy this pet's vibrant nature.
It should keep you entertained.

Gemini:

A Sagittarius is your polar opposite. What you have in common is that you both thrive on activity, and you both like variety. The difference is that your pet is a physical wanderer while you are a mental wanderer.

Cancer:

This pet could seem to be too much of a flit-about for your stay-at-home nature. Its restless spirit can make you nervous. Your Sagittarian pet loves by trying to cheer you up. You might do better with a more emotionally nurturing sign.

Leo:

This is the Huckleberry Finn–Tom Sawyer combo. You two can't help but like each other as your out-looks are so similar. You both agree: If you can't have a good time, it ain't worth doing. This pet could well turn out to be the best buddy of your life.

Virgo:

Your pet's scattered way of going about things could be a little disconcerting to your organized mind. Your pet has a much simpler view of things than you do. You feel slightly out of sync and attracted to this pet's carefree ways at the same time.

Libra:

You both have a knack for making each other feel good. You'll appreciate your Sagittarian's light-hearted approach to life. You can let it out the back door and know that it will be back, because you are the one it loves the most.

Scorpio:

This pet will gladly go off and play when you are in
one of your moods where you'd like to be alone.
When it comes home, it will greet you as it always
does. As long as you are not too possessive, this can
be a compatible match.

Sagittarius:

As long as you both head off in the same direction,
you'll tickle each other to death. Otherwise, it's unlikely you'll ever see each other, because you both
get distracted with what's before you and can easily
forget where home it.

Capricorn:

You'll like your pet's nerve. Your Sagittarian will
try anything with you that you can think of. If you
want to go mountain climbing, your pet will be
right behind you. This pet can also remind you to
laugh more often.

Aquarius:

You two can think up things to do together that no
one else would even imagine. You'll strike out in
bold and new directions that the more faint-hearted
would shudder at. You can bring out each other's
best sense of adventure.

Pisces:

You might find your Sagittarian's actions more
blunt than your gentle ways. It may seem to be too
easily lured away by the other pets in the neighborhood, leaving you feeling unattended and wondering why you got a pet in the first place.

CAPRICORN

BORN: December 22 through January 20
SYMBOL: Goat
RULER: Saturn
ELEMENT: Earth
KEY WORD: "I use"

At first glance your Capricorn pet may seem a little reserved or shy. Actually, it is busy sizing you up. Not overly demonstrative in public, it's not about to warm up to you until after you've paid for it and have it halfway home. Once it knows that you are for real, you really bought it, it's really yours, then you'll understand your initial unconscious attraction to it. It loves you deeply and has a quiet inner strength that will never let you down.

Your Capricorn pet won't be quick to trust, so don't expect any overt displays of affection or interest in its new home for a day or two. It won't bound through the house knocking things over or jump up

on the kids' beds or make a lot of noise in the barn.
It will find a spot out of the way but still in your line
of sight to watch for a while. When it feels secure
that it understands the workings of your family, it
will consider observing what the neighborhood has
to offer. Capricorns do things slowly at first until
they get the hang of things. Then watch out.

It's hard to believe that an animal can plot and
plan, but trust me, your Capricorn pet thinks things
through and always has a reason for everything it
does. Before you know it, your defenseless little
dear will emerge on top of the pile. You can count
on your pet excelling at something, whether it's being the most popular pet in the neighborhood, the
one who can perform the most tricks, or the most
intelligent. Somehow, some way, this pet will stand
out from the crowd and make you proud you own it.

Expect your Capricorn pet to be choosy about
its buddies. This pet is not one to bring home any
strays or try to save any souls. Once it figured out
that you can't change anybody except yourself, it
stopped trying. Live and let live is its motto. Anyway, it's quality, not quantity, that your pet seeks.
Even though your pet will have lots of acquain-
tances (it doesn't want to slight anybody), it will
take its time to make a true friend. It doesn't easily
let someone get close to its feelings. But if you do
win this pet's heart, you'll stay a friend for life. One
thing your pet is not is fickle.

Capricorns don't mind being alone so it isn't a
big deal if you have to be absent for a while. Your
pet was also born reserved so there's no need to
worry about childish fits of rage or destruction.

More likely, you'll never know that your pet is mad at you for leaving it alone. This pet can be awfully stoic. Please don't be fooled by that. Its feelings run deep, and it needs lots of love and affection.

Your pet is fairly easy to train. It takes its studies very seriously. These pets are so conscientious and have such a need to excel that I wouldn't be shocked to see one practicing on its own. They want to do well. Be careful not to criticize your pet in public. Capricorns embarrass easily.

The older the pets get, the younger they look and act. You figure that one out. Maybe they have the secret of life: Save your youth until you're old enough to understand life, then you can have the energy and spirit to enjoy it. Sounds like a good plan to me. So, as far as exercise goes, you may need to coax them a little when they're younger, but once they get the hang of it, they're off and running.

You don't have to wait until your Capricorn grows up to enjoy it. This pet makes a loyal guardian and faithful friend from the very beginning. And it won't ask much from you in return.

Especially Appropriate Names for Your Capricorn:

Citadel	Wile E. Coyote	Mason
Rocky	Surefoot	Elvis
Ol' Man	Emperor	Spencer
Midas	Colonel	Atlas
Top Gun	Bones	Solomon
Champion	Super Ball	Winter
Ambition	Macbeth	Thor
Big Doots	Mr. Dog	Fortune
Forbes	Boss	Opus

Fox	Elspeth	Cashmere
Kaiser	Sable	

How You and Your Capricorn Pet Will Get Along If Your Sign Is:

Aries:

Your Capricorn pet has a mind of its own. If you don't try to boss this pet around, you'll get along better. This pet can be instrumental in showing you how to pace your extravagant energies.

Taurus:

A Capricorn makes a devoted pet for you. It will loyally protect you because it naturally loves you, and because you feed and take care of it so well. You and your pet will enjoy a happy and secure friendship.

Gemini:

You may not know what to make of such a serious pet. A Capricorn thinks before it acts, unlike spontaneous you. But if you are looking for a faithful defender of your home while you are out and about, this is a good choice.

Cancer:

This pet represents your opposite astrological sign. You may feel your pet has its own world and doesn't pay enough attention to you—probably because it's too busy taking over the neighborhood. A little affection will go a long way.

Leo:

You'll like your Capricorn's dignified conduct. This pet will never cause you any embarrassment. Even though you may feel a camaraderie with your pet, when others are around you may also feel slightly competitive toward it, both of you vying for attention.

Virgo:

You will admire this pet's stately manner. You and your pet share very compatible outlooks and interests. You'll like your Capricorn's steady nature, and it will appreciate your reliability. You'll be automatic friends.

Libra:

You may find that your Capricorn pet takes a while to warm up to you. Don't be alarmed. It's just that this pet is more reserved and not always demonstrative. If you can accept its quiet kind of love, you won't feel rejected.

Scorpio:

Of all the signs, Capricorn is most like you. You both make great observers and have deep emotions others don't always get to see. You'll be able to share a closeness of feeling that is enviable. This is a good match.

Sagittarius:

You're just what this pet needs to loosen it up. A Capricorn pet is just what you need to remind you that there are such things as responsibilities. You both can improve and grow from being together.

Capricorn:

You Capricorns can judge each other very harshly and/or be best friends. You both have high standards that you unconsciously impose on each other. That doesn't mean you don't get along. Nobody understands a Capricorn like another Capricorn.

Aquarius:

As Aquarius is also co-ruled by Saturn, Aquarians and Capricorns actually do quite well together. You will keep things interesting for your Capricorn pet, while your pet will help ground you. You'll feel instinctively better by being together.

Pisces:

Your pet's innate ability to take command will help you feel safe and sound. Your soothing ways will ensure that your pet feels well cared for. You'll complement each other very nicely. You and your Capricorn pet will enjoy a lasting and harmonious tie.

AQUARIUS

BORN: January 21 through February 19
SYMBOL: Water Bearer
RULER: Uranus

ELEMENT: Air
KEY WORD: "I know"

The person who coined the phrase "man's best friend" had an Aquarian pet. These pets are born for the sole purpose of being someone's friend. What? You say they're weird though? That's only because they come from another planet. And they prefer being called eccentric, unusual, unique—but not weird. If you are looking for one of a kind, you've found it.

This pet may confuse you at first. You bring it home and it lavishes total attention and affection on you. You think, "This is great. Finally a pet who only has eyes for me." That is, until your partner or child walks in the door and your pet is off, having eyes only for the new arrival. Remember, these pets are humanitarians. They care deeply about everyone they meet. They expect you to realize that *of course* they love you more. But that doesn't mean they can't be kind to others. Oh yeah, I forgot to mention that they're like that with other animals too. They are everybody's friend.

Don't worry about having every pet in the neighborhood camping in your backyard. Aquarians like to visit, and more often than not, they'll be the ones to make the rounds. This way they get to see how others live and what good things they have to eat.

Your Aquarian pet likes to experience the new and different. It also enjoys every sensory pleasure. If your pet does invite the neighborhood over for a bash (it starts innocently enough with one pet being invited; then the pet next door finds out and is hurt and must be invited too, and so on . . .), it won't expect you to have to help with the entertaining. Your pet's idea of entertaining is every pet for itself. Your Aquarian's job is to get all the interesting pets together. Then it's up to each of them to make their own good time. Everything in life should be a jointly shared effort.

Aquarians are pretty easygoing creatures. They roll with the punches. If you leave them alone for longer than usual, they'll simply think you got detained and won't get bent out of shape emotionally. Sometimes those things happen. Of course they won't expect you to get upset either if they leave you a present on the kitchen floor. Sometimes those things happen.

What your pet will bring to your life is a new way of looking at things. If you've always thought of your shoe as just an ordinary shoe, you are in for a magical mystery tour. That shoe can be turned into a place to hide a treasure, or a food dish, or an exotic hat, or a stiff mitten, or a commode (only when you've left your pet alone for too long), or a toy boat to sail in the birdbath. Aquarian imaginations know no limits. They are used to being visionaries and seeing things that others miss.

Another advantage with this pet is that it's a snap to train. Show it once, and voilà, a trained pet. Aquarians catch on very quickly. If you happen to have a slow learner, you might have to show it twice, but that's all. As for exercise, they're much more interested in mental exercise, so you may have to remind them to do a few laps. If you tell them it soothes their nerves and improves their cardiovascular system, they'll be more inclined to go without a fuss. They like anything that smacks of science—though they'd be perfectly happy if they had no bodies at all. It's such a bother to lug it around. The mind is so much more fascinating.

This pet is as close to having a human being in an animal as you're going to get. It seems to know instinctively what you are feeling. It will share your interests happily and always make you feel that you are the most wonderful, exciting person in the world. It will stay your true-blue friend for life. If none of this seems too hard to take, then you've found the pet for you.

Especially Appropriate Names for Your Aquarius

Quirky	Wizard	Star Baby
Oracle	Valentine	Anomaly
Sparky	Antennas	Amadeus
Rebel	Free Spirit	Galileo
E.T.	Gadget	Mr. Spock
Buddy	Gizmo	Eureka
Kilowatt	Lightning	Ozzie
Merlin	Affinity	Maverick
Offbeat	Pal	Quark
Friend	Space Cadet	Galaxy
Radar	Lincoln	

How You and Your Aquarius Pet Will Get Along If Your Sign Is:

Aries:

You'll enjoy your pet's interest in the new and the unusual. As neither of you are ones to sit home and collect dust, you'll share many exciting adventures together. Your pet will make a fascinating companion for you.

Taurus:

An Aquarius pet may be somewhat eccentric for your tastes. This is not a traditional pet, and you won't be able to count on predictable behavior. If you can get used to your pet's multifarious nature, you might even find all that change refreshing.

Gemini:

This pet can even give you a run for your money when it comes to ingenuity and a quick mind. You'll be alternately tickled and impressed by your pet's inventive ways to entertain you. You often make ideal friends.

Cancer:

You may find that an Aquarius pet doesn't give you quite as much personal love and attention as you would like. It can act more as if it belongs to the whole neighborhood than to you. Don't worry about your pet's social ways. It loves you more.

Leo:

This pet is your zodiac opposite. You will either be dazzled by its distinctiveness or baffled by its bizarreness. One thing an Aquarius won't do is leave you feeling indifferent. If you do get along, it will be a long-lasting match.

Virgo:

This pet will help shake up your routine a little bit. Just what you need to keep the cobwebs from growing on your old ways of doing things. You won't exactly know why, but this pet will make an intriguing addition to your life.

Libra:

Nobody will appreciate your charm and innate balance the way an Aquarius pet will. You'll like your pet's sense of concern for others. You and your pet will share a blending of love and friendship that will make others envious.

Scorpio:

You and your pet will have basically different ways of feeling and being. You are more concentrated and singleminded. Your Aquarius is more expansive and open-ended. This may not be the pet for you if you are looking for an intimate bond.

Sagittarius:

Your may never find a more witty and fun combination than you and your Aquarius pet. You can bring out the ridiculous in each other and roll on the floor with mirth and glee. Try not to inflict yourselves on any unsuspecting upright citizens.

Capricorn:

You can't help but like your Aquarius. It brings out the side of you that you're missing—the free spirit who doesn't care what others think. You may feel a bit uncomfortable at first, but after a while you too will be won over, as is everyone else.

Aquarius:

This is one of the few signs that pretty much always like their counterparts. Remember, this is the sign of friendship. You can't help but like each other. Besides, who else is weird enough to understand you? You're often buddies for life.

Pisces:

An Aquarius pet is one of the few who will be able to share your visionary temperament and join along with you. When you need time to yourself, it will keep itself entertained until you pop back in again.

PISCES

BORN:	February 20 through March 20
SYMBOL:	Fish
RULER:	Neptune
ELEMENT:	Water
KEY WORD:	"I believe"

Is that a mirage you think you're seeing? It's probably just a Pisces. There is something otherworldly about these pets. Maybe it's their extraordinary gentleness or their flair for being whatever you need them to be. At any rate, their physical demeanor leans toward the fragile or delicate. Whether they bewitch you with their ethereal charm or evoke your sympathy, they make you want to protect them from the mean, cruel world.

When you get your pet home, you'll automatically find yourself trying to feed it or make sure it's comfortable, all the while wondering why you're fawning over it. These pets have a knack for getting people to do things for them. The quicker you realize your pet won't break, the sooner you'll help it adapt to its new environment. Don't be afraid to throw it out the back door for a while. Nothing will come along and eat it. Your Pisces pet may seem a little disoriented at first, but once it settles in, it will romp and play with the best of them. You'll just have to make an effort not to be overprotective.

Because your Pisces pet is not aggressive, you won't have to worry about it starting any gang wars in the neighborhood. Pisceans are pretty shy and are unlikely to make the undertaking to meet others on their own. They would much rather be at home and listen to music with you. You might even have to take your pet by the paw, or hoof, or whatever and make the initial introductions to others of its kind so that it will make friends. Again, once it does have friends, it acclimates beautifully. Pisceans are very compassionate and caring. But they are also noticeably gullible and easily influenced. So, if you feel the need to be protective, make sure they don't fall in with the wrong crowd. Otherwise you might find yourself bailing out your sweetheart from the pound.

This is another pet who is not a problem to leave alone. You can leave Pisceans indoors or out-

doors, and they'll be perfectly behaved either way.
They'll spend the time you are away in their own
beautiful dream world. These pets are particularly
sensual. You might not want to leave a female outside alone because she'll find it hard to resist a ro-
mantic overture. If you have to leave your pet outside, have it neutered first unless you plan on going
into the breeding business. If you choose to leave
your pet alone in the house while you are gone, it
would appreciate you leaving the radio on. This is
one pet who really loves melodious sounds.

Training your Pisces pet is going to have to be a
gradual process. These pets wilt if you are too stern
with them. Easy does it. They do much better if you
show them what you want them to do first instead
of pushing or pulling them. They want to accommo-
date you in a heartfelt way and will try their
darnedest for you. Oddly enough, for all their reti-
cence and shyness, once you do get them trained,
they often demonstrate star quality. They take
home more than their fair share of ribbons from pet
shows.

Your Pisces pet will play with you when you
want to play, be quiet with you when you want to be
quiet, go for a ride with you when you want to go for
a ride. Your wish is its command. A more gentle and
giving soul you will not find. If you want a pet who
will not cause you any grief and one who will stay
by your side lovingly no matter what your age, take
this shimmering mirage home for your very own.

Especially Appropriate Names for Your Pisces

Lamb	Chameleon	Peppy le Pew
Sarah	Picasso	Cloud
Bernhardt	Zen	Zelda
Orca	Silver Ghost	Woozie
Phantom	Hope	Boatswain
Boo	Fishy	Rainbow
Splash	Flim Flam	Mooch
Flipper	Daffy Duck	Omega
Casper	Jack Daniels	Gabriel
Rapture	Mirage	Mr. Magoo
Dream On	Neptune	Tibet

How You and Your Pisces Will Get Along If Your Sign Is:

Aries:

Your Pisces pet may seem somewhat delicate to you at first. Don't be fooled by its wispy appearance. This pet can call on great staying power when it needs to. It's not aggressive though, so don't expect it to charge when you say charge.

Taurus:

You and your pet will be innately sympathetic to each other. You move to the same rhythms of life and share a gentle, unharried way of going about daily activities. It all gets done by the end of the day. You make natural pals.

Gemini:

You may think this pet has a hard time getting out of its own way. It simply does things differently than you do. If you don't rush your Pisces pet, it will

do a lot better. This pet needs time for day-
dreaming.

Cancer:

This pet was made for you. Your Pisces pet will respond intuitively to your emotional sensitivities.
You'll lavish your pet with tender care and it will
reward you with undying devotion. You've found a
haven in your Pisces pet.

Leo:

You could find a Pisces pet especially entertaining.
It shares your flair for the dramatic. You'll have to
watch what you say and how you treat this pet,
though. It is extremely sensitive and gets crushed
easily.

Virgo:

If you want a pet you can protect and fuss over
while it takes care of you, a Pisces is your pet. This
is your opposite sign. It operates its life by osmosis,
where you rely on details and organization. If you
accept that, this can be a loving match.

Libra:

You and your pet have an artistic temperament in
common. You are also both sensitive to others'
needs. There can be some friction in actually doing
things together since your energy levels are somewhat different. This can translate to moodiness.

Scorpio:

You'll feel instinctively connected to your Pisces
pet. Here's someone with whom you can share all

your secrets and innermost feelings. Days could go by without you seeing anyone, but you won't care because you'll have your best friend with you.

Sagittarius:

First impressions can be deceiving. If you look too quickly, you'll think a Pisces pet doesn't have a sense of adventure. Most likely a Pisces invented one of the dreams you love to follow. This pet isn't weak, just gentle.

Capricorn:

You'll delight in the tender attention a Pisces pet pays to your feelings and needs. This pet will bring out the nurturing side of your nature. You'll both bask in the quiet warmth and caring you give to each other. This often makes a wonderful pair.

Aquarius:

While a Pisces pet may not be quick to take off to parts unknown with you, it will share your dreams and visions. When you do return, your pet will be eagerly waiting to hear all about it.

Pisces:

This pet will immediately understand and easily participate in your flights of fancy. Two birds of a feather—or, in this case, two fish joined together. Others may wonder what you are up to. But no word need be exhanged for you two to know.

4

Everything you always wanted to call your pet...and more

When it comes to choosing pet names, I have found that nothing is sacred. Nothing! People's sense of the truly sublime and the equally truly ridiculous prevail. It seems virtually anything can be and is the source for a pet name. Names come from such diverse areas as figures from history, sports heroes, movie stars, fictional characters, geographic locations, physical descriptions, deceased relatives, living relatives, ex-wives or husbands, food groups, alcohol and beverages, and foreign languages (for some of us, after all, that's the closest we'll get to another country).

Doggie stars are popular, although I was disappointed to see that the Rin Tin Tin and Lassie of my day have been replaced by Benji and Spuds MacKenzie. Oh, how fickle is fame. And kitty stars ranked high for favorite names. Of course, Morris leads the pack, or should I say litter?

Many pets are named for terms of affection, though I wonder what the neighbors of "Poopy Bear," "Snugums," "KissKiss," or "Honey" think when the proud owners stand on the porch bellowing for their pets to come home. How many wives and husbands run home as well, thinking—or hoping—they are being beckoned by their mates?

Pet names also come from flowers and vegetables, outer space, and personality traits. These traits, as you might guess, can be a little daunting. Imagine, for instance, the anxiety of the veterinarian who has to give "Snapper" his booster shots.

Of course, when all else fails, and we can't come up with a name from these varied sources . . . we simply make one up.

I've included additional categories for people who think the trials and tribulations of owning one pet aren't enough and opt for two or three of a kind. These come under the heading of "Tandems and Trios," such as "Sooner" and "Later," "Woofer" and "Tweeter," and "Huey, Luey, and Duey."

You'll notice that I've chosen not to discriminate by labeling certain names as appropriate only for certain animals. I figure whether you have a cat, dog, fish, bird, horse, rabbit, or other, the names are, for the most part, interchangeable. This way your imagination can have free rein. Who's to say you can't name your dog "Kitty" if you feel like it? Certainly not I.

I should also explain why I decided to organize the names serendipitously. I did it partly because I'm a serendipitous kind of person, but mostly because I tried listing them first by category, then alphabetically, by male, female, and "fixed," and every other which way. The names lost their special sound and meaning in a blur of monotony. In their current order (or disorder), the names unexpectedly pop off the page to tickle you—exactly because you don't know what will come next. You'll hear each name as if you are trying it on your own pet.

In using this little compendium, there are a few helpful tips. I've put a line in front of each name so you can put a check next to the ones you like the most. Then you can easily compile these into a list from which you can select your favorite name. You might also keep a clean sheet of paper handy in case my list stimulates you to think up some names of your own. And now, without further ado, enjoy yourself. Occasionally you'll come across a name that will give you a hearty laugh. But more important, if you're looking for a name for your special pet companion, you're sure to find one you that suits you both—perfectly!

____ Yogi

____ Oreo

____ Black Velvet

____ Carey

____ Dandelion

____ Rajah

____ Mouth

____ McDuff

____ B.B.

____ Bunny

____ Runt

____ Frances

____ Hercules

____ Peppy le Pew

____ Snapper

____ Farina

____ Dodger

____ Tar Baby

____ Bedouin

____ Katmandu

____ Pirou

____ Dalby

____ Venus

____ Ulysses

____ Full of It

____ Shammie

____ Dottie

____ Coley

____ Scoobie Doo

____ Taz

____ Moxie

____ Collier

____ Puddles

____ Herb

____ Scrappy   ____ Jubatus
____ Emma   ____ Gad Zukes
____ Coramay   ____ BonBon
____ Jane   ____ Fftt

The entire population of hamsters in the United
States was started by one female with twelve young
imported from Syria in 1938.

____ Muss   ____ Keté
____ Lady Bug   ____ Curly
____ Zsa Zsa   ____ Mickey
____ Freckles   ____ Kara
____ Tarpan   ____ Peaches
____ Buster   ____ Poo Poo
____ Brut   ____ Miyoshi
____ Chi Chi   ____ Panther
____ Shaggy Dog   ____ Cherise
____ Ruby   ____ Bubbly
____ Cloud   ____ Dinah
____ Kate   ____ Simca
____ Walker   ____ Tee
____ Randy   ____ Allie
____ Crazy   ____ Mai Ling
____ Allioop   ____ Lightning
____ Kiesta   ____ Marlee
____ Happy   ____ Anthony
____ Tanner   ____ Bummer
____ Dody   ____ Sparky
____ Jerry   ____ Harry
____ Tish   ____ Tique
____ Darby   ____ Henry
____ Fonzy   ____ Posh
____ Chenille   ____ Cameron

____ Perkins	____ Bitsy Bear
____ Tinka	____ Daisy Mae
____ Tang	____ Cahill
____ Moe	____ Frankie
____ Echo	____ Heather
____ Wile E. Coyote	____ Pudgy
____ Puma	____ Winchester
____ Tar	____ Zebediah
____ Sundown	____ Oats
____ Betsy Ross	____ Andy
____ Butch	____ Goofy
____ Bruce	____ Billy Bob
____ Billy	____ Ubu
____ Tai	____ Oshkosh
____ Branigan	____ Skittles
____ Dagwood	____ Clarissa
____ Kibbles	____ Heidi
____ Tobias	____ Gigi
____ Camee	____ Werner
____ Horse	____ Bandit
____ Alaska	____ Alex

Apart from humans and elephants, whales, dolphins, and porpoises are the most intelligent mammals.

____ Bumper	____ Huckleberry
____ Little Guy	____ Styx
____ Tea	____ Nutmeg
____ Yeoman	____ Little Girl
____ Nick	____ Diamond
____ Zelda	____ Jetter
____ Andrea	____ Chelsey
____ JoJo	____ Bubbles

____ K.C.	____ Tiziano
____ Pepe	____ Homer
____ Mattie	____ Willie
____ Noah	____ Brat
____ Puffer	____ Madam
____ Callahan	____ Thompson
____ Lily	____ Kola
____ Woodstock	____ Luke
____ Prado	____ Scruffy
____ Roxie	____ Burly
____ Fanny	____ Argus

A man goes up to the cage of a parakeet and says,
"Can you talk? Can you talk?" The parakeet gives
him a bored look and answers, "Yes, I can talk. Can
you fly?"

____ Smurf	____ Jade
____ Jackson	____ Paddy
____ Marx	____ Ruger
____ Tambi	____ Boatswain
____ Petunia	____ Skippy
____ Little Lion	____ Kosh
____ Foof	____ Travis
____ Woozie	____ Ruff
____ Spunky	____ Nina
____ Mavis	____ Ponto
____ Kanga	____ Knight
____ Munchie	____ Mortimer
____ She-Ra	____ Ted
____ Beanie	____ Jason
____ Wolfgang	____ Snarf
____ PeeWee	____ Captain
____ Kayo	____ Kristy

_____ Maybe

_____ C.J.

_____ Sherlock

_____ Richelle

_____ Lexi

_____ Stormy

_____ Marbles

_____ Kudos

_____ Woodchip

_____ Allison

_____ L.B.

_____ Jip

_____ Thornton

_____ Shogun

_____ Patty

_____ Kahlua

_____ Pandora

_____ Jet

_____ Ruggles

_____ Skeeter

_____ Chantilly

_____ Tank

_____ Hurly

_____ Joey

_____ Thea

_____ Bugs

_____ Ruskin

_____ Joleen

_____ Twister

_____ Dale

_____ Billie Sue

_____ Averell

_____ Shanda

_____ Flipper

_____ Munchkin

_____ Corky

Bunny grub: green vegetables.

_____ Randy

_____ Camp

_____ Dandy

_____ Maude

_____ Star

_____ Chinky

_____ Tawny

_____ Royal Flush

_____ Paolo

_____ Bull's-Eye

_____ Sport

_____ Sarge

_____ Honey

_____ Theodore

_____ Pinocchio

_____ Spice

_____ Loco

_____ Lady

_____ Tramp

_____ Blackie

_____ Birdie

_____ Nikki

_____ Lucky

_____ Midnight

_____ Sandy

_____ Bosco

____ Dino

____ Cisco

____ Nubbin

____ Nuisance

____ Tundra

____ Sasha

____ Scamper

____ Spike

____ Tony

____ Lola

____ Tippy

____ Princess

____ Sudio

____ Lupu

____ Max

____ Samantha

____ Moussa

____ Dusty

____ Sally

____ Baby

____ Zinger

____ Edgar

____ Sheena

____ Queenie

____ Charlie

____ Molly

____ Kita

____ Rebel

____ Mooch

____ Worthless

____ Barney

____ Tigger

____ Beau

____ Stitches

____ Buttons

____ Lulu

____ BeBe

____ Murdock

____ Rama

____ Cribbet

____ Jalina

____ Pirate

____ Kopen

____ Susie Q

____ Puck

____ Muppie

____ Poker

____ Jemie

____ Corey

____ Montgomery

____ Muggins

____ Huck

____ Piper

____ Kyas

____ Shiner

____ Peachy

____ Marcy

____ Hillary

An ostrich with its head in the sand is just as blind to opportunity as to disaster.

___ Rudy	___ Brenna
___ Sawyer	___ Odie
___ White Fang	___ Roderick
___ Mercer	___ Yvonne
___ Lottie	___ Banjo
___ Gideon	___ Leroy
___ Valiant	___ Helicopter
___ Moby	___ J.J.
___ Krinkle	___ Zebra
___ Jacinda	___ Winks
___ Tuff Stuff	___ Alvin
___ Speedy	___ Omega
___ Delight	___ Quackers
___ Luanne	___ Hermit
___ Northrop	___ Eden
___ Eureka	___ Ripley
___ Denby	___ Fagin

A riddle:
Thirty white horses upon a red hill.
Now they tramp, now they champ, now they stand still.

    (Answer: teeth)

___ Virgil	___ Abbot
___ Sommers	___ Jonathan
___ Kelsey	___ Sphinx
___ Jean	___ Bjorn
___ Bernadine	___ Loverly
___ Calypso	___ Owen
___ Tallulah	___ Xavier

_____ Calvin   _____ Elmo
_____ Rudolf   _____ Thimble
_____ Gerhard   _____ Whirlaway
_____ Kore   _____ Lucretia
_____ Salami   _____ Nolan
_____ Bronson   _____ Petula
_____ Mandolin   _____ Utah
_____ Finnegan   _____ Spumoni
_____ Thomasina   _____ Lewis
_____ Soufflé   _____ Tidbit
_____ Uncle Whiskers   _____ Hortense
_____ Wes   _____ Alissa
_____ Mirage   _____ Caswell
_____ Yardley   _____ Daphne
_____ Dancer   _____ Lady Di
_____ Hippo   _____ Johann
_____ Ultra   _____ Demeter
_____ Wiley   _____ Blythe
_____ Miss Piggy   _____ Gershwin
_____ Nessie   _____ Possum
_____ Sutherland   _____ Lorelei
_____ Dingaling   _____ Zoe
_____ Jaimee   _____ Alsab
_____ Ilanna   _____ Ondine

A big, energetic German shepherd was talking to a
little poodle in the next cage at the kennel. "What's
your name?" asks the poodle. The shepherd shakes
his head. "Not really sure—but I think it's
Downboy!"

_____ Hotshot   _____ Choppers
_____ Uriel   _____ Humph
_____ Sapphire   _____ Vinny

___ Sullivan	___ Clyde
___ Lombard	___ Frisky
___ Elvis	___ Jody
___ Fabian	___ Sophie
___ Salvador	___ Buckets
___ Moppet	___ Judy
___ King Kong	___ Punch
___ Rhea	___ Jessica
___ January	___ Tara
___ Sugah	___ Pup
___ Timothy	___ Velvet
___ Bronson	___ Berry
___ Roberto	___ Seneca
___ Chandra	___ Strawberry
___ Adam	___ Caesar
___ Millicent	___ Rastus
___ Granville	___ Yuri
___ Tinsel	___ Belle
___ Wheeler	___ Stang
___ Quinn	___ Cubby
___ Hiram	___ Sue
___ Twit	___ Ginger
___ Holly	___ Cody
___ Benny	___ Bandit
___ Licorice	___ Taffy
___ J.R.	___ Katie
___ Ben	___ Pepper
___ Buddy	___ Abner
___ Cringer	___ Snoop
___ FiFi	___ Goldie
___ Tuffy	___ Tanya
___ Rainbow	___ Vivo
___ Brindle	___ Pop-Eye
___ Orion	___ Bear

____ Pal	____ Larissa
____ Boots	____ Fiona
____ Bullet	____ Cameo
____ CoCo	____ Truly
____ Turk	____ Dennison
____ Merry Weather	____ Jewel
____ Big Foot	____ Carlin
____ Fast Lane	____ Vanessa
____ Sprite	____ Myron
____ Ali Baba	____ Hagar
____ Norton	____ Ursula
____ Yates	____ Sully
____ Bismarck	____ Caitlin
____ Lamb Chop	____ Lyrics
____ Keira	____ Joel
____ Sundance	____ Hilary
____ Xerox	____ Valencia
____ Ansel	____ Marshall
____ Ode	____ Albert
____ Rosemond	____ Zadie
____ Truffles	____ Kenny
____ Calamity	____ Wakefield

One yuppie to another: I've decided not to board my dog this summer. Who needs it? I'll give him a Visa card and let him get along on his own.

____ Dillie	____ Honeybee
____ Saki	____ Gersham
____ Rosalind	____ Flame
____ Irene	____ Cassidy
____ Zebulon	____ Roxanne
____ Jacobine	____ Gray Friar
____ Brett	____ Camille

____ Maynard	____ Bo Diddly
____ Harmony	____ Spencer
____ Tilda	____ Upton
____ Pogo	____ Rolly
____ Fluff Puff	____ Griselda
____ Molasses	____ Carmen
____ Susanna	____ Ogden
____ Nobie	____ Wolf
____ Hunter	____ Kodak
____ Gabriel	____ Rochelle
____ Vanilla	____ Efram
____ Wallis	____ Cheetah
____ Alphonse	____ Daffy
____ Auralie	____ Lorenzo
____ Hastings	____ Niccolo
____ Trudy	____ Keenan
____ Vladimir	____ Trina

A man renamed his horse Flattery because it gets
him nowhere.

____ Spear	____ William
____ Dinsmore	____ Ludwig
____ Quicksilver	____ Newt
____ Miranda	____ Bonus
____ Sax	____ Ruby
____ Huntington	____ Sanborn
____ Dumbo	

Relatives are the worst friends, said the fox as the
dogs took after him.

____ Vernon	____ Payton
____ Rochester	____ Geraldine

____ Jacques	____ Noelle
____ Slalom	____ Jocelyn
____ Emerson	____ Sondra
____ Maxwell	____ Willa
____ Alonzo	____ Lil
____ Wesley	____ Thomas
____ Sonny	____ Kalamazoo
____ Robinson	____ Radcliff
____ Phil	____ Winner
____ Odette	____ Aloha
____ Tuesday	____ Saxton
____ Cecie	____ Herbert
____ Deiter	____ Trinka
____ Mr. Magoo	____ Ping Pong
____ Fearless	____ Yosha
____ Saloma	____ Jamaka
____ Charlotte	____ Boogie
____ Delta	____ Deacon
____ Alpha	____ Frosty
____ Yoshi	____ Tut
____ Josephine	____ Walnut
____ Bradford	____ Tibet
____ Thorndike	____ Dudu
____ Buttermilk	____ Arabesque
____ Ilsa	____ Atlas
____ Natalie	____ Mad Hatter
____ Vashti	____ Ike
____ Kameko	____ Wizard
____ Tabasco	____ Mr. Ed
____ Lazarus	____ Omar
____ Dario	____ Banana
____ Carina	____ Whoopi
____ Trapper	____ Jonah
____ Brooke	____ Malcolm

____ Kahu	____ Elsa
____ Duchess	____ Brighton
____ Toby	____ Brady
____ Ginny	____ Penny
____ Dickens	____ Bull
____ Marmalade	____ Boo
____ Tweetie	____ Gordy
____ Justin	____ Squirt
____ Comanche	____ Kali
____ Winter	____ Thaddeus
____ Gumdrop	____ Dena
____ Autumn	____ Radar
____ Tibs	____ Helli
____ Elmer	____ Leander
____ Tusk	____ Babbie
____ Silver Ghost	____ Gamma
____ Lint	____ Raquel
____ Mercedes	____ Feather
____ Beef	____ Wilma
____ Solomon	____ Sancho
____ Flynn	____ Zandra
____ Basil	____ Jean Luc
____ Dennis the	____ Aila
Menace	____ Pancho
____ Arizona	____ Natala
____ Nicholas	____ Campbell
____ Wendell	

Never try to catch two frogs with one hand.

____ Trep	____ Yuma
____ Whittaker	____ Jan
____ Fax	____ Leilani
____ Scout	____ Patches

_____ Gabe

_____ Raoul

_____ Trevor

_____ Dagmar

_____ Keziah

_____ Ezra

_____ Shoshone

_____ Hadley

_____ Malarkey

_____ Snow

_____ Desiree

_____ Elissa

_____ Sahi

_____ Hector

_____ Madison

_____ Alban

_____ Barnum

_____ Nibbles

_____ Cactus

_____ Solo

_____ Weegie

_____ Fortune

_____ Theobold

_____ Vaughn

_____ Jacoba

_____ Latham

_____ Pharaoh

_____ Snoopy

_____ Melly

_____ Fang

_____ Aardvark

_____ Sassy

_____ Gidget

_____ Wicket

_____ Jogaty

_____ Jingles

_____ Suzie

_____ Booty

_____ Duke

_____ Pooh

_____ Trixie

_____ Jake

_____ Beauford

_____ Sheba

_____ Gretchen

_____ Honest

_____ Deirdre

_____ Ting

_____ Schnapps

_____ Ranger

_____ Rusty

_____ Fraulein

_____ Gizmo

_____ Jazz

_____ Marmaduke

_____ Eeyore

_____ Hub

_____ Crow

_____ Shadow

_____ Jasper

_____ Rocky

_____ Snuggles

_____ Patch

_____ Jenny

_____ Tracy

_____ Daisy

_____ Bambi

_____ Crosby

____ Brandy	____ Wei Wei
____ Julie	____ Westbrook
____ Roger	____ Ukulele
____ Tabatha	____ Fox
____ Thor	____ Siegfried
____ Kimo	____ Babar
____ Merlin	____ Georgette
____ Wraba	____ Ozzie
____ Isaiah	____ Calliope
____ Dugan	____ Dana
____ Nell	____ Twine
____ Amadeus	____ Sunny
____ Parrie	____ Krypton
____ Natty	____ Telex
____ Reuben	____ York
____ Trey	

In the United States, cats outnumber dogs as household pets 56,500,000 to 51,000,000.

____ Valerie	____ Ledo
____ Jaffa	____ Be-Bop
____ Lark	____ Hsing Hsing
____ Boris	____ Mae
____ Iago	____ Alta
____ Orville	____ Phelps
____ Remy	____ Quasar
____ Dervin	____ Neddie
____ Xena	____ Chandra
____ Troy	____ Whirling Dervish
____ Fuzzy	____ Sven
____ Talbot	____ Keriann
____ Vince	____ Enoch
____ Henny Penny	____ Sherwood

____ Jimini	____ Jessalyn
____ Maribel	____ Macaroni
____ Amil	____ Idette
____ Pablo	____ Nadia
____ Gabby	____ Cara
____ Orleans	____ Wyatt
____ Ryan	____ Suds
____ Dex	____ Kaiser
____ Sutton	____ Elijah
____ Trent	____ Tango
____ Ferris	____ Zero
____ Sloan	____ Hilton
____ Yoshiko	____ Mahala
____ Vale	____ Lisette

"Peanuts" is the world's most popular comic strip with "Garfield" running second.

____ Amory	____ Bigwig
____ Patience	____ Georgia
____ Olaf	____ Remington
____ Carter	____ Dumpling
____ Waite	____ Tully
____ Fernando	____ Stacy
____ Zig Zag	____ Heddi
____ Jenica	____ Mamie
____ Steffie	____ Libby

Horse food: oat cuisine.

____ Anton	____ Barnabus
____ Parker	____ Frazzle
____ Imogene	____ Copper
____ Galen	____ Simon

- ___ Harlequin
- ___ Missy
- ___ Sadie
- ___ Muffin
- ___ Chelsea
- ___ Ziggy
- ___ Mandy
- ___ Panda
- ___ Lucky
- ___ Chip
- ___ Sly
- ___ Satch
- ___ Browny
- ___ Perrin
- ___ Razzmatazz
- ___ Lenny
- ___ E.T.
- ___ Hart
- ___ Tag
- ___ Hans
- ___ Smokey
- ___ Toast
- ___ Mitzy
- ___ Betsy
- ___ Cindy
- ___ Barley
- ___ Benjamin
- ___ Punkin
- ___ Docker
- ___ Kelly
- ___ Wiggles
- ___ Mack
- ___ Spark Plug
- ___ Blue

- ___ Buffy
- ___ Champion
- ___ PeeWee
- ___ Kia
- ___ Jessie
- ___ Stolie
- ___ Avalon
- ___ Sherman
- ___ Daryl
- ___ Salvadore
- ___ Gumby
- ___ Kareem Abdul
- ___ Stinko
- ___ Jarvis
- ___ Rags
- ___ Tasha
- ___ Fart
- ___ Bijoux
- ___ Redneck
- ___ Drew
- ___ Stewart
- ___ Keiko
- ___ Fru Fru
- ___ Tinkerbell
- ___ Jeremiah
- ___ Lloyd
- ___ Palmer
- ___ Griffin
- ___ Drusilla
- ___ Neal
- ___ Rafferty
- ___ Swifty
- ___ Utopia
- ___ Evan

_____ Tildie   _____ Bebe
_____ Holbrook   _____ Isadora
_____ Marcello   _____ Calder
_____ Alexis   _____ Grits
_____ Ducky   _____ Winthrop
_____ Carney   _____ Stillman
_____ Oui   _____ Kama
_____ Pluto   _____ Fairly
_____ Carla   _____ Videl
_____ Wrinkles   _____ Janel
_____ Tricia   _____ Leland
_____ Ethan   _____ Stutter
_____ Sweet Pea   _____ Hugo
_____ Herbie   _____ Randall
_____ Marilee   _____ Ileanne
_____ Anya   _____ Beelzebub

When Joe's horse got sick, he put some powder
in a pipe and stuck the pipe into the horse's mouth,
with his mouth on the other end, ready to blow. But
the horse blew first.

Was the powder strong?

Strong? Joe sneezed twice after he died.

_____ Uppity   _____ Albon
_____ Styles   _____ Pascal
_____ Honora   _____ Dulcy
_____ Dun   _____ Woodrow
_____ Ramsey   _____ Turtledove
_____ Ira   _____ Titus
_____ Father O'Grady   _____ Vivien
_____ Sheldon   _____ Rene
_____ Honda   _____ Hollis
_____ Masher   _____ Addie

___ Pez	___ Joel
___ Geoffrey	___ Black Jack
___ Freya	___ Junior
___ Jerome	___ Joba
___ Leif	___ Joy
___ Whitman	___ Gandolf
___ Van Gogh	___ Precious
___ Jess	___ Rattler
___ Carmel	___ Bimbo
___ Naomi	___ Chipper
___ Greer	___ Sach
___ Page	___ Turbo
___ Virginia	___ T.C.
___ Janet	___ Rambo
___ Laverne	___ Mutley
___ Beven	___ Asia
___ Gallagher	___ Miles
___ Oren	___ Snowflake
___ Ulric	___ Beetle
___ Fitzgerald	___ Keena
___ Sebastian	___ Tudor
___ Dolph	___ Pierre
___ Nevada	___ Woofie
___ Lainey	___ Spuds
___ Babs	___ Milo
___ Gracie	___ Toes
___ Wallis	___ Turkey
___ Homer	___ Maggie
___ Margo	___ Heidi
___ Adolpho	___ Ebony
___ Obie	___ Puncho
___ Grendel	___ Bridget
___ Otis	___ Mugs
___ Amber	___ Sniglet

____ Bowser   ____ Cleo
____ Rag Bag   ____ Nathan
____ Misty   ____ Fred
____ Rufus   ____ Nashua
____ Sirus   ____ Gwendolyn
____ Heathcliff   ____ Essa
____ Mimi   ____ Yule
____ Digger   ____ Horatio
____ Bogus   ____ Gill
____ Samson   ____ Iodine
____ Tootsie   ____ Sabina
____ Scotty   ____ Virgo
____ Willow   ____ Algernon

I shot an elephant in my pajamas. How he got in my
pajamas, I'll never know. —Groucho Marx

____ Gladys   ____ Françoise
____ Washburn   ____ Kerry
____ Messie   ____ Tybalt
____ Sheehan   ____ Porky
____ Rhett   ____ Magdalena
____ Big Ben   ____ Ingrid
____ Hedda   ____ Cyrus
____ Mendel   ____ Pepita
____ Ansel   ____ Yolanda
____ Selma   ____ Janey
____ Minx   ____ Lawrence
____ Arnold   ____ Whit
____ Gus   ____ Haillie
____ Petronia   ____ Lamar
____ Carson   ____ Gina
____ My Dream   ____ Philippe
____ Van   ____ Blaze

____ Rafael	____ Tyne
____ Hamlin	____ Winnie
____ Theo	____ Callie
____ Easter	____ Janine
____ Urchin	____ Leonard
____ Woolite	____ Big Bird
____ Heeby Jeeby	____ Governor
____ Mead	____ Quartz
____ Attila	____ Sharpie
____ Portia	____ Frenchie
____ Isabelle	____ Zola
____ Whitey	____ Uno
____ Thorpe	____ Helinka
____ Shani	____ Manuel
____ Wynn	____ Athena
____ Ferdinand	____ Patrice
____ High Jinks	____ Rue
____ Lancelot	____ Waverly
____ Briana	____ Eli
____ Gazelle	____ Udall
____ Charise	____ Dominic
____ Faun	____ Hilda

I got a haddock herring that tuna blow "salmon
chanted eel-ing" and, upon my sole, he did it on por-
poise.

____ Marissa	____ Bonzo
____ Arlo	____ Gerhardt
____ Percy	____ Daria
____ Kasimir	____ Fidel
____ Sapphire	____ Tige
____ Farrel	____ General Lee
____ Lattimer	____ KiKi

____ Scarlet   ____ Kitty
____ Splash   ____ Little Bit
____ Chester   O'Honey
____ Izzy   ____ Sir
____ Zodiac   ____ Tyrone
____ Franny   ____ Amy
____ Bangles   ____ Tiger
____ Moses   ____ Dollie
____ Moonshine   ____ Jack
____ Cupcake   ____ Josh
____ Bud   ____ Tamu
____ Targhee   ____ Fluffy
____ Kaanapali   ____ Weebe
____ Jetson   ____ Elspeth
____ Marcus   ____ Pearl
____ Kermit   ____ Silverhawk
____ Tally Ho   ____ Bosley
____ Elton   ____ Stockton
____ Morgan   ____ Charlie Brown
____ Tedi   ____ Todo
____ Skunk   ____ Trigger
____ Felix   ____ Popcorn
____ Cotton Candy   ____ Friendly
____ Sable   ____ Puddings
____ Whiskey   ____ Hopper
____ Tyler   ____ Josie

Dog Emporium: Groomingdales.

____ Vicki   ____ Cecil
____ Hara   ____ Weston
____ Maharani   ____ Yipper
____ Gustave   ____ X-tra
____ Broomtail   ____ Raleigh

___ Pollyanna	___ Silvan
___ Zenda	___ Felicity
___ Jemima	___ Helen
___ Liberty	___ Kassia
___ Pet	___ Iona
___ Gunner	___ Buzzsaw

If fish were as big as stories told about them, fish-mongers would sell sardines in garbage cans.

___ Enrico	___ Marnie
___ Zanie	___ Abe
___ Julian	___ Guy
___ Hyacinth	___ Harlow
___ Remus	___ Orchid
___ Ferd	___ Val
___ Lolita	___ Patsy
___ Tess	___ Orson
___ Nipper	___ Halona
___ Devon	___ Lila
___ Idalia	___ Thelma
___ Nada	___ Mona
___ Willa	___ Vance
___ Sizi	___ Gifford
___ Madrid	___ Umeko
___ Chuckles	___ Barnaby
___ Humphrey	___ Nanette

The paws that refreshes.

___ Hutt	___ Jolie
___ Rover	___ Winona
___ Hope	___ Garnet
___ Melba	___ Myrtle

___ Burgess	___ Mercy
___ Cupid	___ Finn
___ Robbie	___ Mike
___ Howie	___ Whiskers
___ Gilbert	___ Levi
___ Ebenezer	___ Cagney
___ Janot	___ Lindsey
___ Cheshire	___ P.J.
___ Dazzle	___ Kayak
___ Osborn	___ Nightmare
___ Hetti	___ Kiley
___ Reid	___ Q-tip
___ Sid	___ Spot
___ Jozef	___ Jovi
___ Cashmere	___ Packy
___ Harrison	___ Purr
___ Claus	___ Rondack
___ Sal	___ Tanker
___ Harpo	___ Puff
___ Octavius	___ Moose
___ Gusto	___ Cookie
___ Teresa	___ Nana
___ Hermie	___ Buster
___ Reese	___ Quiche
___ YoYo	___ Meow
___ Polly	___ Soot
___ Hazel	___ Quincy
___ Sergeant	___ Teary
___ Adler	___ Simone
___ Wilton	___ Scrapper
___ Ilona	___ Candie
___ Harman	___ Buck
___ Crocker	___ Lars
___ Rae	___ Agatha

___ Meggy	___ Speck
___ Cheyenne	___ Zeke
___ Prince	___ Lucy
___ Terri	___ Taco
___ Bozo	___ Cassie
___ Ubi	___ Gucci
___ Skipper	___ Kaleeda
___ Shane	___ Harold
___ Natchez	___ Leona
___ Ashes	___ Trix
___ Muffy	___ Gene
___ Champ	___ Austin
___ Caddyshack	___ Hewitt
___ Me-too	___ Gipper
___ Shawna	___ Quail
___ Sooner	___ Hannibal

Papa Bear: "Who ate my porridge:"
Mama Bear: "Who ate my porridge?"
Baby Bear: "Urp!"

___ Cotton Tail	___ Merrielle
___ Muriel	___ Winifred
___ Yucca	___ Hobby
___ Fitz	___ Jere
___ Hank	___ Linus
___ Nelson	___ Bea
___ Rafe	___ Romeo
___ Toto	___ Edison
___ Horace	___ Jude
___ Paul	___ Ace
___ Vanna	___ Odel
___ Clay	___ Hutton
___ Sidney	___ Gilda

____ Bullet	____ Albie
____ Walker	____ Toots
____ Indy	____ Unity
____ Troy	____ Rocker
____ Ross	____ Haskel
____ Zeb	____ Dirk
____ Fluff	____ Raff
____ D.C.	____ Olin
____ Clover	____ Veda

Animal who takes the longest to leave the nest:
man.

____ Samara	____ Juan
____ Alexina	____ Harper
____ Wright	____ Paxton
____ Crispin	____ Royce
____ Ezekiel	____ Yale
____ Vel	____ Dizzie
____ Flo	____ Lydia
____ Snugums	____ Byron
____ Gerard	____ Topaz
____ Hogan	____ Irv
____ Rainie	____ Colin
____ Heloise	____ Walton
____ Edsel	____ Hobard
____ Chloe	____ Silvio
____ Zared	____ Meryl
____ Jama	____ Kittiwink
____ Monroe	____ Lauren
____ Hale	____ Amara
____ Oswell	____ Cairo
____ Rosabel	____ Margarita

If you ain't the lead dog, the scenery never changes.

___ Velma   ___ Poco

___ Velma	___ Poco
___ Catalina	___ Tiffany
___ Dmitri	___ Snap
___ Rory	___ Chatamack
___ Elroy	___ Duncan
___ H. M. Flycatch	___ Carma-Pete
___ Woody	___ Zack
___ Rex	___ Sunshine
___ Matilda	___ Crackers
___ Sonya	___ Amos
___ Spaz	___ Bobbi
___ Felicia	___ Sam
___ Wayne	___ Mackenzie
___ Sniffy	___ Rossi
___ Ozymandias	___ Sounder
___ Skooter	___ Alf
___ Dixie	___ Zebu
___ Bo	___ Oscar
___ Stirling	___ Ralph
___ Joshua	___ Busch
___ Gandhi	___ Winston
___ Morris	___ Joker
___ Angelina	___ Nelly
___ Nugget	___ Wooper
___ Buddha	___ Maude
___ Teddy Bear	___ Garfield
___ Stymie	___ Sanford
___ Beast	___ Florio
___ Bob	___ Giles
___ Maggy	___ Todd
___ Rex	___ Irwin
___ Later	___ Horton

____ Rosanna   ____ Belinda
____ Charity   ____ Paint
____ Jay   ____ Clarence
____ Turtle   ____ Hux
____ Lotus   ____ Sinclair
____ Beatrice   ____ Lorri
____ Walter   ____ Ram
____ Yves   ____ Gino
____ Judd   ____ Nigel
____ Amani   ____ Harriet
____ Townsend   ____ Frazier

Longest lived pet: animate—tortoises have lived 150
years; inanimate—pet rocks; some are estimated to
live millions of years.

____ Amelia   ____ Vivie
____ Uriah   ____ Giovanni
____ Hassle   ____ Bess
____ Critter   ____ Santana
____ Donder   ____ Mommy
____ Zena   ____ Casey
____ Reba   ____ Nunzio
____ Nika   ____ Squat
____ Quentin   ____ Khaki
____ Ingmar   ____ Weezie
____ Taggard   ____ Hobo
____ Monica   ____ Popsicle
____ Satin   ____ Shep
____ Mighty Mouse   ____ Buford
____ Ivor   ____ Ned
____ Electra   ____ Nova
____ Conner   ____ Bert
____ Huxley   ____ Brogan

- ____ Mickey Ran
- ____ Mittens
- ____ Delilah
- ____ Flossie
- ____ Cheri
- ____ Binkley
- ____ Doc
- ____ Nippy
- ____ Winny
- ____ Schecky
- ____ Otto
- ____ Murphy
- ____ Chiquita
- ____ Pugsie
- ____ Rocko
- ____ Oh Boy
- ____ Kyle
- ____ Kam
- ____ Blondie
- ____ Leo
- ____ Shiloh
- ____ Minou
- ____ Clem
- ____ Nadine
- ____ Winky
- ____ Lady Brittany
- ____ Misty Ann
- ____ Opal
- ____ Frank
- ____ Marlboro
- ____ Maverick
- ____ George
- ____ Boomer
- ____ Tammy
- ____ Gonzo
- ____ Strider
- ____ Tabby
- ____ Chocolate Mousse
- ____ Trouble
- ____ Cooper
- ____ Germaine
- ____ Java
- ____ Kirsten
- ____ Morie
- ____ Rutherford
- ____ Igloo
- ____ Benton
- ____ Gilroy
- ____ Cass
- ____ Murray
- ____ Larry
- ____ Elvira
- ____ Hymie
- ____ Wanda
- ____ Cullie
- ____ Sean
- ____ Jules
- ____ Fielding
- ____ Peg
- ____ Rozelle
- ____ Mopsy
- ____ Rona
- ____ Fergie
- ____ Omega
- ____ Zipp
- ____ Crow
- ____ Saul
- ____ Anders

___ Holt	___ KissKiss
___ Reggie	___ Madge
___ Giselle	___ Eliza
___ Jinx	___ Haldon
___ Rosita	___ Ian
___ Vick	___ Hattie
___ Nissa	

Pets capable of learning a form of communication
understandable to humans: Parrots can mimic
speech, and dolphins and apes have learned sign
language.

___ Justin	___ Shalom
___ Fergus	___ Jocko
___ Lianne	___ Filbert
___ Mab	___ Lani
___ Glynis	___ Thad
___ Tomasa	___ Riley
___ Huntley	___ Darcy
___ Regan	___ Hamil
___ Hershel	___ Clarie
___ Bali	___ Radburn
___ Gaston	___ Janka
___ Fern	___ Findley
___ Madelyn	___ Cicely
___ Stu	___ Hardy
___ Hurdle	___ Rider
___ Hester	___ Trinket
___ Vallie	___ Asta
___ Dasher	___ Jania
___ Patton	___ Joachim
___ Osgood	___ Harlan
___ Halsey	___ Cissy

____ Rad	____ Nubs
____ Hamlet	____ Leila
____ Igor	____ Mildred
____ Nate	____ Rust
____ Wilona	____ Hermosa
____ Etna	____ Pinky
____ Mariel	____ Ophelia
____ Courtney	____ Hal
____ Arrow	____ Zora
____ Gwenith	____ Isa
____ Box	____ Oxford
____ Van Dyke	____ Reeves
____ Pasha	____ Selby
____ Hussein	____ Allegra
____ Roanna	____ Bernie
____ Silas	____ Henrietta
____ Mia	____ Mardi Gras
____ Avis	____ Corbin
____ Viola	____ Quiver
____ PomPom	____ Red
____ Calico	____ Glynis
____ Zollie	____ Laika
____ Mace	____ Mabel
____ Glenda	____ Vera
____ Dora	____ Noel
____ Ruthie	____ Warden
____ Bertram	____ Rachel
____ Iris	____ Jana

Eat like a bird? Not if you're on a diet. Birds eat at least half their own weight in food every day.

____ Alfie	____ Milly
____ Chap	____ Oneida

___ Drum	___ Ivy
___ Beulah	___ Reanna
___ Hernando	___ Binky
___ Cal	___ Blinker
___ Zorana	___ Megan
___ Nye	___ Bilbo
___ Vixen	___ Shaker
___ Tempest	___ Dempsey
___ Apache	___ Tassie
___ Bruno	___ Togo
___ Twinkie	___ Jasmine
___ Sabrina	___ Reggie
___ Sara Lee	___ Tommy
___ Bonnie	___ Cugeran
___ Neimo	___ Truman
___ Farraday	___ Robin
___ Trinket	___ Rising Sun
___ Quark	___ Tristan
___ Suzette	___ Laser
___ Lincoln	___ Koto
___ Andiamo	___ Ella
___ Yahoo	___ Shannon
___ Forrester	___ Midget
___ Curtis	___ Sugar
___ Wolf	___ Pretzels
___ Rio	___ Stubby
___ Keats	___ Baby Cakes
___ Koukla	___ Judy
___ Woolly	___ Glowworm
___ Jelly Bean	___ Raggedy
___ Forbes	___ Inez
___ Babe	___ Tangles
___ Reckless	___ Conlon
___ Punky	___ Norman

___ Flint	___ Grimalkin
___ Coral	___ Wells
___ Vida	___ Prancer
___ Elsie	___ Tally
___ Jeremy	___ Irisa
___ Granger	___ Ollie
___ Lou	___ Selena
___ Rica	___ Lonnie
___ Micah	___ Terence
___ Helga	___ Grover
___ Emile	___ Ramone
___ Flyball	___ Biff
___ Doria	___ Charlene
___ Beryl	___ Jim

To talk much and arrive nowhere is the same thing
as climbing a tree to catch a fish. —Chinese proverb

___ Adlai	___ Sigmund
___ Vincent	___ Washout
___ Chastity	___ Colby
___ Prentice	___ Juliet
___ Fossie	___ Erin
___ Iren	___ Richard
___ Reb	___ Mitch
___ Lucas	___ Golda
___ Dublin	___ Bowie
___ Seth	___ Innis
___ Hinda	___ Leon
___ Olivia	___ Fury
___ Tad	___ Sheffie
___ Virtue	___ Hugh
___ Chevy	___ Dylan
___ Blitzen	___ Rum

____ Shelly	____ Whitney
____ Dudley	____ Prissie
____ Inga	____ Alanna
____ Sheffield	____ Jilly
____ Adria	____ Ruddy
____ Felt	____ Nora
____ Hubard	____ Conrad
____ Lyle	____ Sheridan
____ Tate	____ Enid

Advertisement: Husband says either he or puppies must go. Puppies are half golden retrievers, playful, cute. Husband is cross and unsympathetic. Your choice. Free.

____ Mohammed	____ China
____ Josiah	____ Dutch
____ Fable	____ Fido
____ Irma	____ Tacita
____ Telly	____ Alexander
____ Les	____ Sneakers
____ Dexter	____ Tree
____ Fuji	____ Thunder
____ Aldo	____ Sniffles
____ Hum	____ Damien
____ Bones	____ Dallas
____ Guinevere	____ Spooky
____ Rhanee	____ Penelope
____ Mitri	____ Mira
____ Bumpkin	____ Leia
____ Minx	____ DB
____ Arrow	____ Lady Slipper
____ Erika	____ Rita
____ Yang	____ Stella

___ King	___ Prudence
___ Vito	___ Talia
___ Maze	___ Elias
___ K2	___ Miguel
___ Shea	___ Jove
___ Rosie	___ Letisha
___ Tipper	___ Weber
___ Wookie	___ Lester
___ Schultz	___ Templeton
___ Tina	___ Gopher
___ Abigail	___ Rhonda
___ Trump	___ Algernon
___ Tickles	___ Seti
___ Melissa	___ Pockets
___ Snowball	___ Mouser
___ Wishbone	___ Asterix
___ Tiki	___ Sassafras
___ Gretel	___ Kilimanjaro
___ India	___ Bulova
___ Rockefeller	___ Nuthin
___ Bailey	___ Underdog
___ Frodo	___ Taylor
___ Moss	___ Jordan
___ BJ	___ Coralee
___ Cee Cee	___ Noreen
___ Ed	___ Isaac
___ Rosco	___ Do-Wop
___ Pedro	___ Shelby
___ Sara	___ Fellini
___ Nigel	___ Aztec
___ Boone	___ Tex
___ Alden	___ Prue
___ Russ	___ Guthrie
___ Wayland	___ Leopold

____ Granite   ____ Belafonte
____ Short Stop   ____ Mouse Tse Tung
____ O'Brien   ____ Cyclone
____ Beckett   ____ Seldom Fed
____ Orca   ____ Dragonslayer
____ Kiwi   ____ Stop Dammit

Advertisement: Energetic 3 1/2-month old puppy
seeks intelligent woman to date 30-year-old owner.
Interest in travel, sports, and good food recommended. Good sense of humor and puppy treats required.

____ Cat Ballou   ____ Camber
____ Monsignor   ____ Varsi
____ Nerd   ____ Indiana
____ Dream On   ____ Mushnik
____ Sir Love-a-Lot   ____ Rafer
____ Choo Choo   ____ Biter of Enemies
____ Tackleberry   ____ Kilkenny
____ Raisin   ____ Denzel
____ Jabba   ____ Skywalker
____ Redmond   ____ Slugger
____ Quirky   ____ Hathaway
____ Pink Panther   ____ Wack-a-do
____ Popples   ____ Thundercat
____ My Man Godfrey   ____ Citadel
____ Smedley   ____ Stony
____ Sackett   ____ White Tiger
____ Jailbird   ____ Absurd
____ Virginia Woof   ____ Offbeat
____ Brigette Bar-dogg   ____ Jangle
____ Obadiah   ____ Downey
____ Jabber   ____ Waggles

| ____ King Pin | ____ Abaca |

Two out of three critters can fly.

____ Shenandoah	____ Cleveland
____ Hansel	____ Logan
____ Daffodil	____ Carly
____ Little Jean	____ Shatzi
____ Ichabod	____ Cuddles
____ Enos	____ Opus
____ Hammer	____ So Big
____ Sham	____ Ewok
____ Lukie	____ Baron
____ Tinker	____ Togo
____ Mindy	____ Gimper
____ Kichi	____ Tux
____ Bianca	____ Willy
____ Gypsy	____ Natasha
____ Bunsie	____ Tucker
____ Brutus	____ Hershey
____ Skeeter	____ Grunt
____ Travers	____ Demi
____ Butterscotch	____ Maxwell
____ Molson	____ Hanna
____ Ol' Man	____ Jupiter
____ Pebbles	____ Watson
____ Joe	____ Porsche
____ Apricot	____ Partly
____ Peanut	____ Rupert
____ Holmes	____ Cheri
____ Angel	____ Lugar
____ Hansel	____ Sammy
____ Bugsy Malone	____ Susala
____ Jukebox	____ Kimba

___ Mabry   ___ Nanny
___ Tobacco   ___ Tram
___ Yakker   ___ Zenith
___ Waldo   ___ Lagger
___ Fair Play   ___ Gadget
___ Clancy   ___ Dorkie
___ Macbeth   ___ Lobo
___ Peddler   ___ One Step
___ Quiggles   ___ Schnook
___ Jacob   ___ Kabul
___ Hound Doggie   ___ Dody
___ Jigsaw

Q: What do you get if you cross a hummingbird with
a doorbell?
A: A humdinger.

___ Dude   ___ Lamb
___ Absalom   ___ Oracle
___ Greaser   ___ Scuttle Butt
___ Chaucer   ___ Tipsey
___ Epoch   ___ Rambler
___ Moby-Dick   ___ Falcon
___ Hot Dog   ___ Chessie
___ Persia   ___ Wang Poo
___ Rommel   ___ North Star
___ Mister   ___ Kimbo
___ Tuxedo   ___ Bentley
___ Enforcer   ___ Anheiser
___ X Ray   ___ Omelet
___ Cid   ___ Montezuma
___ Domino   ___ Scamp
___ Jeep   ___ High Fi
___ Lop-Sing   ___ Phantom

____ Ornery
____ Spooker
____ Tamarack
____ Entrepreneur
____ BooBoo
____ Deputy
____ Emerald
____ Adonis
____ Gremlin
____ Xanadu
____ Xmas
____ Jacques
____ Fellow
____ Bumblebee

____ Two by Four
____ Liebchen
____ Saucy
____ Raven
____ Inca
____ Picasso
____ Quintella
____ Sugarfoot
____ Flea Bag
____ Blossom
____ Padre
____ Egghead
____ Bootsie
____ Thane

A duck has three eyelids on each eye.

____ PomPom
____ Les the Man
____ Ferocious
____ Dilly
____ Cartwheel
____ Klem
____ Peppermint
____ Morticia
____ Gunga Din
____ Crackerjack
____ Cappie
____ Jumper
____ Nookie
____ Tim
____ Hound
____ Jam
____ Kong

____ Wilbur
____ Kojak
____ Tika
____ Cinders
____ Gwen
____ Tarama
____ K9
____ Anastasia
____ Fella
____ Harvey
____ Moon
____ Gobi
____ Goliath
____ V-8
____ Victoria
____ Sherina
____ Jackie

____ Crystal   ____ Killer
____ Conan   ____ Pounce
____ Topper   ____ Trinka
____ Buster Brown   ____ Panda
____ Lazy   ____ Hudson
____ Tilly   ____ Grace
____ Fritz   ____ Katrina
____ John Paul   ____ Cricket

Q: How do insects communicate?
A: With buzzwords.

____ April   ____ Flymo
____ Mackie   ____ Lucia
____ Packey   ____ Sally Ann
____ AJ   ____ Lady Grace
____ Sergio   ____ Webster
____ Zorro   ____ Verne
____ Pixie   ____ Jersey
____ Duster   ____ Pilfer
____ Rascal   ____ Little Devil
____ Yukon Jack   ____ Scout

Don't buy a camel that shakes while sitting. It's a
good bet its front legs are bad.

____ Priscilla   ____ Kiss
____ MacPherson   ____ Hobbit
____ Baboon   ____ Ruffles
____ Cutie   ____ Mandrake
____ Puddin   ____ Hopsing
____ Tripper   ____ Vodka
____ Tumbleweed   ____ Wee Willie
____ Peter Pan   ____ Andromeda

___ Rounder

___ Pooh Bear

___ Galaxie

___ Booger

___ Emmett

___ Serendipity

___ Tulip

___ Oh No

___ Junebug

___ Animal

___ Shorty

___ Zen

___ Lover

___ Monique

___ Undertaker

___ Numero Uno

___ Scarf

___ Fireball

A dog who lets you gently pull its toes apart should be safe with children.

___ Gawky

___ Eskimo

___ Snagglepuss

___ Streak

___ DeeDee

___ Luscious

___ Sunshine

___ Old Timer

___ Pampero

___ Kim

___ Gong

___ Babo

___ Can Do

___ Nomad

___ Rabbit

___ Pig Pen

___ Yankee

___ Waggs

___ Dice

___ Molly Sue

___ Jade

___ Fancy Dance

___ Achilles

___ Bruiser

___ Mr. Ling

___ Packer

___ Sabbath

___ Zonker

___ Xylophone

___ Fang

___ Gunter

___ Luna

A storm is on the way if your cows lay down, act
fidgety, or head for the barn.

____ Naughty	____ Grabber
____ Scott	____ Paco
____ Lance	____ Laughs-a-lot
____ Inky	____ Grizzly
____ Nautilus	____ Jammys
____ Aimless	____ Bitzy
____ Pris	____ Buttercup
____ Ling Soo	____ Charcoal
____ Badger	____ Jimmy
____ Colonel	____ Ava
____ Epsilon	____ Monday
____ Oleander	____ Bingo
____ MacGregor	____ Sweetfeet
____ Seeker	____ Jessabelle
____ Odin	____ Aramé
____ Harley	____ Salmon
____ Khaki	____ Fletcher
____ Egad	____ Mocha
____ Sentar	____ Andrew
____ Quest	____ Bo Duke
____ Monster	____ James
____ Arf	____ Pat
____ Diablo	____ Flicka

Bumper sticker: It's ten o'clock. Do you know where
your gerbil is?

____ Jigger	____ Kit
____ Chucky	____ Austin
____ Lacey	____ JD
____ Pete	____ Marty

___ Ninja	___ Ad-lib
___ Pita	___ Iliad
___ Topsy	___ Dapper Dan
___ Minka	___ L'eggs
___ Starsky	___ Pegasus
___ Plato	___ Scorpio
___ Alyosha	___ Olive Oyl
___ Buckwheat	___ Rip
___ Chauncy	___ Speckles
___ Cheech	___ Philo
___ Lad	___ Jaguar
___ Schnitzel	___ Burma
___ Thumper	___ Enigma
___ Dickie	___ Donkey
___ Kat	___ Fat Albert
___ Taurus	___ Bacon
___ Ciara	___ Hulk
___ Major	___ Midas
___ Pale Face	___ Kingston
___ Mokey	___ O'Henry
___ Kleiner	___ Ramrod
___ Misfit	___ Scrappie
___ Luigi	___ Smallfry
___ Chinlee	___ Oblio
___ Seymour	___ Illusion
___ Peeper	___ Big Boy
___ Eeek	___ Aries
___ Groucho	___ Parka

A quart container will hold about 1,000 crickets, give or take a few.

___ Saber	___ Laura
___ Xenia	___ Frisco

____ Beauty   ____ KoKo
____ Goose   ____ Pal
____ Betelguese   ____ Smallie
____ Oblong   ____ Umber
____ Shastra   ____ Fascination
____ Taj   ____ Candler
____ Valentino   ____ Ergo
____ Wellington   ____ Mama
____ Meesha   ____ Gangster
____ Ambrosia   ____ Chee Chee
____ Eagle Eye   ____ Loner
____ Hoppy   ____ Norman

Glass bottom boat for rent: so fish can see how big
the fellow was they got away from.

____ Perdy   ____ Necessity
____ Redhot   ____ Lonestar
____ Slim Jim   ____ Kannin
____ Unicorn   ____ Oneway
____ Zaki   ____ Slinky
____ Pansy   ____ So Shy
____ Airplane   ____ Whippet
____ Cap   ____ Onyx
____ Levi   ____ The One 'n' Only
____ Fawn   ____ Bamma
____ Demetrius   ____ No Name
____ Beer   ____ Meeshon
____ Chocolate Chip   ____ Garbanzo
____ Ecuador   ____ Eclipse
____ Papa Bear   ____ Carnie
____ Yuck   ____ Bell
____ Wimpy   ____ Panzer
____ Son   ____ Roy

____ Zandu

____ Tiny Tim

____ Paso

____ Mousie

____ Jitterbug

____ Hop Sing

____ Laddie

____ Higgins

____ Speck

____ Tory

____ Magic

____ Kip

____ Ransom

____ Napoleon

____ McKay

____ Caleb

____ Pippin

____ Mischa

____ Smitty

____ Foofer

____ Valentine

____ Squeak

____ Ditty

____ Archie

____ Destiny

____ Hamilton

____ Christi

Sign on a fence: "Don't worry. Our ATTACK dog doesn't bite (very hard)."

____ Pippin

____ Mel

____ Cy

____ Striker

____ Casper

____ Spanky

____ Sugar Babe

____ Smiley

____ Lambert

____ Minny

____ Tycho

____ Furbin

____ Lunatic

____ Flanders

____ Suki

____ Pooch

____ Althea

____ Dillon

____ Hurricane

____ Sylvester

____ Monkey

____ Sweetie

____ Yank

____ Ginger Snap

____ Ishtar

____ Kelo

____ Jack Frost

____ Apollo

____ Kirby

____ Midnight Ride

____ Stephanie

____ Maxine

___ Pookie   ___ Marco Polo

Cocker spaniels top the list of most popular dogs.
Poodles are second. Labrador retrievers are third.

___ Dingbat   ___ Albatross
___ Beethoven   ___ Fish
___ Criton   ___ Pax
___ High Sox   ___ Snert
___ Pebbles   ___ Karma
___ Snickers   ___ Tom Cat
___ Tao   ___ Yonder
___ Uncanny   ___ Winner
___ Zippy   ___ Needles
___ Pears   ___ Kavik
___ Manaka   ___ Fuzz Ball
___ Gator   ___ Curlie
___ Dooley   ___ Admiral
___ Czar   ___ Kshama
___ Belle   ___ Looser
___ Nosy   ___ High Octane
___ Oodles   ___ Target
___ Sparkle   ___ Snip
___ Tarzan   ___ Biddie
___ Tattoo   ___ Dingo
___ Elbe   ___ Fixation
___ General   ___ Jennifer
___ Keeper   ___ Lotto
___ Elan

If your cat rubs against your feet in the morning, it probably wants to stay inside. If it nudges your face, you'd better let it out.

____ Meenie	____ Zed
____ Pert	____ Kong
____ Snoodle	____ Eldorado
____ Teaser	____ Cat
____ Undo	____ Big Foot
____ Yoko	____ Germ
____ Pilgrim	____ Leslie
____ Grubber	____ Pickle
____ Carrie	____ Sonja
____ Aftermath	____ Teddy
____ Bambini	____ Zellar
____ Jiggs	____ Mergatroid
____ Melanie	____ Blazer
____ Puss	____ Gunther
____ Sox	____ Jock
____ Y Not	____ O'Leary
____ Nemesis	____ Terry
____ Albino	____ Unruly
____ Bloomer	____ Bowder
____ Elisha	____ Snookums
____ Finny	____ Sawasi
____ Pico	____ Windsor
____ Spottie	____ Yellar
____ Tether	____ Rapture
____ Wrangler	____ Peridia
____ Nappy	____ Oswald
____ Obsession	____ Kipper
____ Snuff	____ Otherwise
____ Teek	____ Friend
____ Wobbles	____ Sweet Thing

____ Ruffian   ____ Jaywalker
____ Zany   ____ Pauper
____ Tangerine   ____ Geronimo
____ Hear Ye   ____ Dumdum
____ Paws

If your pet thinks you're the greatest, don't seek a second opinion.

____ Einstein   ____ Elmore
____ Buzz   ____ Babette
____ Aesop   ____ Chico
____ Twitter   ____ Poppi
____ Indigo   ____ Zanella
____ Flower   ____ Muskrat
____ Dooby   ____ Infidel
____ Thing   ____ Scrounge
____ Knapsack   ____ Kessie
____ Dirty Dog   ____ Mac
____ Bone   ____ Alamode
____ Cosby   ____ Precious
____ Tenderfoot   ____ Scuttles
____ Rasputin   ____ Tiny
____ Looney Tune   ____ Shabu
____ Duquessa   ____ Fleece
____ Sammy Boy   ____ Bojangles
____ Big Deal   ____ Hop-a-long
____ Acorn   ____ Nebula
____ Yonkers   ____ Nedwick
____ Turp   ____ Benji
____ Hush Puppy   ____ Salt
____ Gambler   ____ Slowpoke
____ Cyrano   ____ Puddles
____ Jeopardy   ____ Orphan

____ Gorilla ____ Jimbo

____ Drake   ____ Pistol

Largest cat: Siberian tiger—eleven feet long. Smallest cat: Rusty spotted cat of India—twenty-five inches long.

____ Spock	____ Jill
____ Stuffy	____ Alpine
____ Tetons	____ Flutter
____ Violet	____ Shanti
____ Yeoman	____ Pong
____ Early Bird	____ Red
____ Sweet Peeps	____ Curious
____ Storm	____ Zipper
____ Uncle Sam	____ Tippan
____ Yokel	____ Flip
____ Kashmir	____ Whistlin' Dixie
____ Earmuff	____ Mozart
____ Georgie	____ Augie
____ Luscious	____ Ringo
____ Susie Q	____ Eric
____ Spectrum	____ Sissy
____ Rabbi	____ Friday
____ Umpire	____ Nudge
____ Zeno	____ Scissors
____ Hutch	____ Kite
____ Sunny Boy	____ Claudia
____ Sinbad	____ Starlight
____ Treetops	____ Bogart
____ White Shadow	____ Schuyler
____ Mutt	____ Doodle

Most animals move their underjaws, except the
crocodile.

____ Blarney	____ Ivan
____ Beauregard	____ Spirit
____ Amanda	____ Funny Face
____ Annabelle	____ Tippet
____ Duffy	____ Fibber
____ Tracy	____ Blunder
____ Ricky	____ Gung Ho
____ Zephyr	____ Pepsi
____ Tibia	____ Stumpy
____ Chinook	____ Underfoot
____ Phoebe	____ Xenon
____ Soogie	____ Kindle
____ Rickety	____ Snookie
____ Kahuna	____ Faction
____ Keech	____ Baboo
____ Rodney	____ Ebon
____ Cendra	____ Goober
____ Nanook	____ Zardoz
____ Phoenix	____ Affection
____ Sambo	____ Baxter
____ Scooper II	____ Kanaka
____ Titan	____ Obnoxious
____ Buff	____ Trooper
____ Lickety-Split	____ Warlock
____ Devlin	____ Jogger
____ Dawn	____ Little One
____ Pia	____ Sting
____ Annie	____ Adept
____ Jeb	____ Capricorn
____ Kendel	____ Dominique
____ Tequila	____ Nuzzle

The world's horse population is estimated to be 75 million.

_____ Santa

_____ Rowdy

_____ Musket

_____ Kira

_____ Posie

_____ Fox

_____ Amelia

_____ Ping

_____ Spade

_____ Dynamite

_____ Lassie

_____ Jambrosia

_____ Sabra

_____ Sailor

_____ Lopsie

_____ Magnum

_____ Eclair

_____ Banner

_____ Careful

_____ Slick

_____ Po

_____ Faith

_____ Kirk

_____ Myra

_____ Bart

_____ Checkers

_____ Sierra

_____ Brie

_____ Cinnamon

_____ Oz

_____ Imp

_____ Camie

_____ Sage

_____ Reagle Beagle

_____ Poopy Bear

_____ Guido

_____ Marigold

_____ Angie

_____ Sushi

_____ Mignon

_____ Sancho

_____ Panchez

_____ Gray

_____ Pouchette

_____ Alec

_____ Raur

_____ Bodean

_____ Fran

_____ Aleister

_____ Abby

_____ Newton

_____ Hoka

_____ Onna

_____ Ashley

_____ Chance

_____ Nutmeg

_____ Tom

_____ Sambucca

_____ Pitch

_____ Zachary

_____ Snuffles

_____ Hoover

___ Mint	___ Lemon
___ Tess	___ Eager
___ Lizzie	___ Neechi
___ Tashi	___ Unanimous
___ Puddy Tat	___ Shaggy
___ Ernie	___ Sexi
___ Razz	___ Otto
___ Tia	___ Tangie
___ Lovey	___ Dillion
___ Bubba	___ Shag
___ Scat	___ Umber
___ Pokey	___ Ocelot
___ Oliver	___ Scorpion
___ Herman	___ Affinity
___ Silver	___ Fiend
___ Sybil	___ Ming
___ Nutsie	___ Weasel
___ Selina	___ Shah
___ Rerun	___ Random
___ Zachariah	___ Shaft
___ Seven-Up	___ Barf

The richest cat was left a $250,000 estate by its owner.

___ Cream	___ Terk
___ Fantasy	___ Shamu
___ Kadabra	___ Taboo
___ Peeve	___ Zing
___ Spats	___ Elroy
___ Weed	___ Jaws
___ Kato	___ Niko
___ Beacon	___ Stinker
___ Egypt	___ Voucher

____ Paddington

____ Hex

____ Busch

____ Nonnie

____ Old Yellar

____ Slim

____ Yen

____ Wheatsworth

____ Nerf

____ DoDo

____ Clancy

____ Pretty Boy

____ Tiddle

____ Streaker

____ Meling

____ Alfalfa

____ Kettle

____ Omen

____ Tiggs

____ Useless

____ Liggie

____ Gusto

____ Little General

____ Omission

____ Stickler

____ TooToo

____ Zeus

____ Chuck

____ Emperor

____ Flander

____ Nipper

____ Jonas

____ Coon

____ Kicker

____ Puka

____ Bragg

____ Emir

____ Porridge

____ Subtle

____ Uppity

____ Licker

____ Gingerbread

____ CooCoo

____ Melody

____ SuSu

____ Tike

____ Nettle

____ Arcadia

____ Kahn

____ Nimbus

____ Psyche

____ Swanky

____ Yours Truly

____ Brendie

____ Cosmo

____ Dumpster

____ Little Girl

____ Pug

____ Stinger

____ Ember

____ Nobbin

____ Toodles

The oldest horse on record lived to be sixty-two years old.

____ Snipper	____ Rasha
____ Pip	____ Macho
____ Jargon	____ Kid
____ Gambit	____ Fleetwood
____ Champagne	____ Eaglet
____ Neeka	____ Pookie
____ Pop	____ Sprint
____ Tetra	____ That's Enough
____ Ceo	____ Chancellor
____ Elixir	____ Dippy
____ Odessa	____ Alexia
____ Uncommon	____ Youngster
____ Zotz	____ Squeegee
____ Thief	____ Condor
____ Keesh	____ Jesse James
____ Bramble	____ Ellie
____ Coffee	____ Porker
____ Sweetie Pie	____ Tonto
____ Potsey	____ Officer
____ Fleet	____ Giggles
____ Buns	____ Chief

The most prevalent domesticated bird is the chicken.

____ Sooty	____ Stripes
____ Christmas	____ Christopher
____ Eunine	____ Flapper
____ Jet Eye	____ Kelso

The most talkative parrot has a vocabulary of about a thousand words.

_____ Argos	_____ Chocolate
_____ U Turn	_____ Zoomer
_____ Squeekie	_____ Strutter
_____ Toad	_____ Arnie
_____ Brewer	_____ Cornie
_____ Top Kat	_____ Pun
_____ O'Malley	_____ Kibbitzer
_____ Nobel	_____ Equinox
_____ Chandler	_____ Brock
_____ Escapade	_____ FuFu
_____ Gin	_____ Jiffy
_____ Kilowatt	_____ Craggy
_____ José	_____ Glider
_____ Artemus	_____ Froggie
_____ Omnibus	_____ Cyrus
_____ Toga	_____ Astor
_____ Butter	_____ Coven
_____ Esoteria	_____ Fluster
_____ Noodles	_____ Orbit
_____ Punchy	_____ Sunset
_____ Tootsie Pop	_____ Nod

The fastest land animal is the cheetah, which can run at 70 mph.
The fastest marine animal is the sailfish, which can swim at 68 mph.
The fastest flying animal is the peregrine falcon, which can reach speeds of 217 mph.

_____ Aquarius	_____ Bushy
_____ Crankcase	_____ Esquire

_____ Freda   _____ Osaka
_____ Trace   _____ Toy
_____ Little Boy   _____ Zee Bart
_____ Summer   _____ Avatar
_____ Putsie   _____ Torch
_____ Osiris   _____ Noggin
_____ Glacier   _____ Goat
_____ Fuchsia   _____ Puzzle
_____ Chica   _____ Ching Ling
_____ Euphrates   _____ Fuzz Buzz
_____ Gobbles   _____ Girl
_____ O'Rourke   _____ Euphoria
_____ Psycho   _____ Otz
_____ Tooli   _____ TiTi
_____ Frangipani   _____ Paloma
_____ Luther   _____ Hazel
_____ Fiver   _____ Sweet Socks
_____ Westy   _____ Cairn

Tandems

_____ Tom & Jerry   _____ Felix & Oscar
_____ Kanga & Roo   _____ Popeye & Olive
_____ Spic & Span   Oyl
_____ Cupcake &   _____ Lady & Tramp
       Cookies   _____ Minnie & Mickey
_____ Chip & Dale   _____ Chili & Beans
_____ Sooner & Later   _____ Mutt & Jeff
_____ Ip & Dip   _____ Punch & Judy
_____ Bonnie & Clyde   _____ Five & Ten
_____ Boogey & Woogey   _____ Zeus & Apollo
_____ Sylvester &   _____ Ipso & Facto
       Tweetie   _____ Gable & Lombard
_____ Big Foot & Little   _____ Laurel & Hardy
       Foot

- Napoleon & Josephine
- Dr. Jekyll & Mr. Hyde
- Beetle & Bailey
- Huntley & Brinkley
- Sticky & Wicket
- Porgie & Bess
- Woofer & Tweeter
- Heckle & Jeckle
- Dutch & Shultz
- Hoot & Holler
- Ace & Deuce
- Cheech & Chong
- Bread & Butter
- Tai & Chi
- FiFi & FuFu
- Frank & Stein
- Amos & Andy
- Double & Trouble
- Casper & Wendy
- Whipper & Snapper
- Sonny & Cher
- Itsie & Bitsie
- Fred & Wilma
- One Step & Two Step
- Salt & Pepper
- Humpty & Dumpty
- Zeus & Hera
- Howdy & Doody
- Lovie & Dovey
- Scuttle & Butt
- David & Goliath
- Pitter & Patter
- Sugar & Spice
- Peter & Pan
- Hurly & Burly
- Mork & Mindy
- Abbott & Costello
- Rock & Roll
- Do Wop & Be Bop
- Flatt & Scruggs
- Laverne & Shirley
- Itch & Scratch
- Smith & Wesson
- Gin & Tonic
- Day & Night
- Nip & Tuck
- Up & Down
- George & Gracie
- Pebbles & BamBam
- Ping & Pong
- Smoke & Fire
- Eager & Beaver
- Snoopy & Woodstock
- Duke & Duchess
- Zig & Zag
- Rodgers & Hammerstein
- Tutti & Frutti

____ Frick & Frack

____ Lenny & Squiggy

____ Hill & Dale

____ Beanie & Weenie

____ Hansel & Gretel

____ Sun & Moon

____ Ozzie & Harriet

____ Yin & Yang

____ Fluff & Puff

____ Chilly & Willy

____ Okey & Dokey

____ Prince & Princess

____ AC & DC

____ Abra & Cadabra

____ Russian &
        Roulette

____ Puss & Boots

____ Pins & Needles

____ Fibber McGee &
        Molly

____ Barbie & Ken

____ Rocky &
        Bullwinkle

____ Barnum & Bailey

____ Dagwood &
        Blondie

____ Li'l Abner &
        Daisy Mae

____ Snow & Storm

____ Slim & Jim

____ Prince & Pauper

____ Beanie & Cecil

____ Ruff & Tumble

____ Hatfield & McCoy

____ Egad & Gad
        Zooks

____ Black & White

____ Coke & Pepsi

____ Hide & Seek

____ Natasha & Boris

Trios

____ Curly, Moe, &
        Larry

____ Muffy, Buffy, &
        Duffy

____ Huey, Louie, &
        Dewey

____ Tom, Dick, &
        Harry

____ Fu, Man, & Chu

____ Koukla, Fran, &
        Ollie

____ Shake, Rattle, &
        Roll

____ Roger, Over, &
        Out

____ Rikki, Tikki, &
        Tavi

____ Faith, Hope, &
        Charity

____ Sasha, Pasha, &
        Tasha

____ Groucho, Harpo,
        & Chico

____ Larry, Daryl, &
        Daryl
____ Ready, Willing, &
        Able
____ Winkin, Blinkin,
        & Nod
____ Georgie, Porgie,
        & Puddin Pie
____ Wee, Willie, &
        Winkie

____ Petunia, Tulip, &
        Daffodil
____ Veni, Vidi, & Vici
____ Alvin, Calvin, &
        Melvin
____ Bibbity, Bobbity,
        & Boo
____ Amo, Amas, &
        Amat

5

Anthology of animal expressions, or how our pets have named us

This work would not be complete without including some of the generous contributions that our pets have made to the English language. Down through the centuries, for as long as people have had pets, it's been common practice to interlace lively and animated conversation with descriptive references to animals. It seems we love to compare ourselves and others in new and inventive ways to the four-legged and winged species.

Just think how often we call upon the name of some animal to conjure up vivid images to help explain an elusive concept. Then, of course, there are many people who get their nicknames from the animal kingdom instead of vice versa. We expect a man nicknamed "Bull" to have massive shoulders and a short, thick neck regardless of whether or not his given name is Alfonse. Psychologists call this form of transference animal envy. Ah yes, the desire to lead a dog's life . . . .

I've included some of the more frequently used sayings. Some meanings have become muddled through overuse or misuse so I've taken the liberty of clarifying them. You'll also find a brief history of origin along with the correct interpretation, so you can confidently use or understand the myriad contexts in which these animal expressions color our speech. The following stories are straight from my horse's mouth.

Albatross
An albatross is a large bird that, once landed, has an extremely difficult time getting airborne again without a long runway. If you have an albatross around your neck, you've got a problem that you can't get away from and can't do anything about. Or you've got a thing for very unique and very large jewelry.

As Poor as Job's Turkey
Job didn't have any turkeys. So if you are compared to Job's turkey, one can only guess how poor is poor. Only the tax man knows for sure. Or in Job's day, the ax man.

At One Fell Swoop
This refers to birds of prey capturing their dinner with one dive. Doing something in one fell swoop is to accomplish a task in one single, successfully completed action. It can also represent an action that is done quickly and ruthlessly, such as "He lopped off its head in one fell swoop."

To Badger
"The little boy badgered his mother for a cookie." *(See also* to bug.) Badgering is just a bigger and more persistent form of bugging, unless we're talking about Watergate; then bugging is bigger. Specifi-

cally, "badger" means to worry or wear the person out until you get your way. Badgers are also kind of ugly. So if someone calls you a badger, you might have cause to be insulted.

Barking Up the Wrong Tree

This expression comes from coon dogs treeing a raccoon until their masters could catch up. But the cool, calm, collected raccoon would simply hightail it over through the next trees and be gone. If you are barking up the wrong tree, you are either looking for the wrong answer to a problem or the full moon has strange effects on you.

Like a Bat Out of Hell

If you've ever seen bats fly out of caves, you know that they do so with great commotion and at brisk speeds. In the good old days of the Inquisition, bats were associated with witches and dark cave openings were thought to be doorways to hell. Today, if you are going like a bat out of hell, it is very likely that you are traveling in your car at a great speed and scaring the people you're passing as you blow their doors in. And probably they are cursing you to go to where bats come from.

Bats in Your Belfry

If you prefer the shorter version—batty. The term refers to people who are thought to have a lot of air space between their ears so that even if they had an idea, it would rattle around like startled bats trying to find their way out of a belfry. If you have bats in your belfry and you don't own a church tower, it's probable that you are considered to be a little crazy.

A Bee in One's Bonnet

This expression is actually quite old. No one calls hats bonnets anymore. The accurate interpretation of this phrase refers to being obsessed with an idea or being slightly dotty. Contrary to the dictates of fashion, it does not mean that bees, doubling as stick pins, are the latest rage in decoration for your Easter hat.

A Bird in the Hand

. . . "is worth two in the bush," as the saying goes. The thinking here is that it's better to keep less and have something sure than to go after more and possibly wind up with nothing. You often get this well-meaning advice from people when you tell them you have a new idea or want to start a new business. The way I look at it, if you've figured out how to get a bird in your hand, you're probably also smart enough to figure out how to get the two in the bush.

Black Sheep

In the old days, farmers viewed black sheep as worthless because there were too few to provide enough black wool to market. Plus the black wool didn't take the old dyes. So they were considered to be bad luck. If you hold this dubious honor in your family, you are looked upon as being the trouble-maker who brings disgrace. But once ostracized, you have the advantage of not having to spend a fortune on Christmas presents.

To Buffalo

Buffaloes loved a fight and were notoriously hard to kill. These massive hulks would charge at hunters at up to fifty miles an hour, often with bullets bouncing off their heads like ricocheting peas. The buffaloes would then die of laughter seeing the terrified hunter take off like a bat out of hell. Today, "to buffalo" means to intimidate or scare off someone by a display of power or force before the person realizes what's happened.

Bug

Bug expressions are almost as prolific as bugs themselves. We call someone "bug-eyed" whose eyeballs protrude, causing a permanent expression of surprise. "Bug juice" is another name for any beverage where the alcohol content is more important than taste. A "bug" also means something that has a defect. "To bug someone" connotes that you are annoying them. A "bug" such as the type installed by the FBI is a phone wiretap. To "bug out" is an army expression for a hasty retreat or moving purposefully anywhere without a purpose.

Bull in a China Shop

The obvious disparity of Ferdinand and Noritaki gives away the key here. It indicates that one is acting clumsily in a delicate situation, with damage expected as the result. Somebody should tell this to the Merrill Lynch ad people.

Bull's-Eye

This is the little black center of a target. It happens to be about the size of a bull's eye. To "hit the bull's eye" means that you've made a direct hit, often meaning that you've accomplished something that requires skill. Or you like to play a risky game of hitting the bull's eye and seeing if you can make it over the fence before the bull catches up and tosses

you over. I know of at least one gold medal sprinter
who built up his speed this way.

Busy Bees
Bees have to visit ten million flowers to make just
one pound of honey. I can assure you that's longer
than an eight-hour work day. It takes dedication,
grit, fortitude . . . and a mindless, manic energy
for repetitious tasks. Sounds like a job for R2D2. As
a consolation, if someone does comment on your in-
dustriousness by calling you a busy bee, you can
always say, "How sweet it is."

A Cat with Nine Lives
Cats are known to be particularly agile and able to
get out of any kind of scrape mostly intact. This is
especially so if its owner happens to be a five-year-
old boy who likes to drop kitty from high places to
see how many times it can land on its feet. If you
are said to have nine lives, it's obviously because
you haven't met up with that five-year-old.

Cat Scan
An intense mind probe by a psychic cat, sometimes
resulting in a nosebleed for the victim. Or Comput-
erized Axial Tomography, which X-rays soft tissues

of the body. Either way, they are both something to be avoided if at all possible.

Curiosity Killed the Cat
In all the years I worked for a vet, I never saw anyone bring in a dead cat killed by curiosity. I've seen 'em done in by cars, dogs, and miscellaneous others. This is just a silly expression, with no basis in fact, used by the same folks who believe in the bird-in-the-hand theory. It has come to be a polite way of being told you're too nosy for your own good.

Chicken Feed
Our economical forefathers fed their chickens chopped up, small pieces of grain whose quality was too poor for any other use. Today the term applies to small change (nickels and dimes), or what's left of your income after Uncle Sam takes his share.

Cock and Bull Story
Cocks and bulls are unlikely pairings, which gives rise to its meaning as a story that has been extravagantly embellished or is just plain not true. Perhaps the cock and bull would be more true to form as the designations for Democrat and Republican politicians. Somehow it seems more appropriate than the donkey and elephant.

Cooked Goose
Geese are hard to cook correctly because of their fat content. They come out either too greasy or too dry. So if you are the average goose cooker, what you are doing won't turn out the way you plan and you'll wind up with something that gets you into trouble with the goose eaters. That is to say, if your goose is cooked, you're in hot water too.

Coon's Age

This expression is a reference to time, often used by people who have no sense of it. Their idea of telling time by a wristwatch is something like half-past a freckle and a hair. If someone tells you that they haven't seen you in a coon's age, that means you've been missing for about thirteen years.

Until the Cows Come Home

Again, another expression of time where people didn't know a Seiko from a sow's ear. If you have to wait until the cows come home, plan on being up until about four in the morning when they come in to be milked. As most people aren't that patient, this expression has come to mean waiting forever for something that will take forever to happen.

Crazy as a Loon

Loons are rather unique in their ability to emit sounds heretofore unheard of in the light of day. Tapes of their blood-curdling cries, possessed wailings, and demonic laughter could be used for soundtracks of some of your favorite spine-tingling horror movies. Because loons seem to go from soulful cries to hysterical laughter for apparently no reason, they've been likened to the mentally unstable. If you are called crazy as a loon, you are either a heavy metal rock singer or you are quite insane; the two behaviors often are indistinguishable.

Cry Crocodile Tears

Crocodiles can't cry because they have no tear ducts. In old myths they were thought to attract their prey by making crying sounds. When the gullible victim came close enough to see what was wrong, the crocodile would snatch it up and eat it for dinner. The expression alludes to the use of hypocritical or pretended sorrow to get what you want. If you cry crocodile tears, your eyes water with joy as you eat, or you are insincere and a little ruthless in abusing others' sympathy.

As the Crow Flies

This is supposed to be a measurement of distance between two places by a straight line in the air versus the winding way of traveling by roads. This suggests that crows fly in a straight line, which should equal the shortest distance between two points. Actually, this was a joke played on the white man by an Indian who has asked to remain anonymous. Crows don't fly straight. They circle like any other birds of prey or scavengers. To an Indian this means going nowhere fast.

Eat Crow

What the white man did when he found out the Indian was pulling his leg. Some say this was to show the Indian a thing or two, although today's meaning has evolved into meaning a display of forced humility.

Cry Wolf

What the shepherd boy did for amusement and to attract company. Those sheep can get awfully boring. His plan was twofold: one, as already mentioned, was to get someone to talk to whose response was other than *baaa;* two, was to make sure that by the time the wolf did come, everyone else would not, thereby ensuring the demise of all his fluffy charges. He was then free to go merrily on his way. Today it pertains to someone who raises false alarms, not unlike those smoke detectors that repeatedly go off in the kitchens of bad cooks.

Dead as a Dodo

The dodo, also known as *Didus ineptus,* was a large flightless bird that was so heavy it could barely fly. It became extinct in 1681 after large-scale slaughter by Mauritian colonists who used dodos as food for their animals. Today, being dead as a dodo suggests that the subject is hopelessly stupid, or that the idea is so bad it's unthinkable and will never get off the ground. Or that you've gone all the way of all good dodos and have died from being overweight and out of shape, with no surviving relatives.

Every Dog Has His Day

If you are Asian and you are a dog having your day, you are celebrating your birthday in the Year of the Dog. If you are not Asian and you are a dog having your day, you are enjoying a brief period of luck or honor in your otherwise dull and meaningless existence.

Don't Change Horses in the Middle of the Stream

Since horses were the only means of transportation in the old days, this was the warning mothers gave their children about not fooling around on their

steeds in any rivers on the way to school. Today the
warning has changed to telling children to look before crossing the road, your basic common-sense adage told to people too young or immature to have
developed any adages of their own. Then there is
also the interpretation of not changing an idea or
candidate halfway through a campaign or crisis.
Again, your elementary words to the not terribly
swift.

Don't Look a Gift Horse in the Mouth
Same thing as not sniffing a gift fish. They are both
ways of telling how old the critter is. This is considered to be an ungrateful and ungracious thing to do
since it implies that you think something is wrong
with your visitor's offering. The correct etiquette of
accepting gifts is to wait until after the gift giver
leaves before you do that.

Go Hog Wild
An old farm expression that means to act wildly
excited for any known or unknown reason. Some
believe its origin is in the old country fairs, where a
common event was chasing the greased pig. The hog
would go wild, squealing about, as men would try to
get a grasp by diving on it. Every time a man got his
arms around the pig, it was so slippery that it would
just shoot out, fly through the air, hit the ground,
and keep on running, and everyone was duly entertained. So much for the good ol' days.

A Fish Out of Water
This has a similar meaning to the lesser known
"fish up a tree." Of course, once a fish is out of water, it really doesn't matter where you put it, or

what you do with it, as it expires rather quickly.
Luckily, if someone refers to you as a fish out of
water, the outcome is not so literal. It just means
you don't know your ass *(see:* derivative of horse and
donkey) from your elbow.

Knee-High to a Grasshopper
To stand up to the tibia of a grasshopper is no mean
feat. You have to be all of one millimeter to three
centimeters tall. It gives new meaning to the expression "short stuff." The reference is usually
made about oneself when telling a childhood anec-
dote to indicate that you were once young and little
too. This is not to be confused with L'Eggs Knee-
Highs to a Grasshopper, which is their new division
for knee-high stockings for the very short.

In the Doghouse
Where you tell your husband's friends they can find
him when he's been bad. Where you tell your dog's
friends they can find him when your husband isn't
occupying his domicile.

To Henpeck
What the domineering wife does to her husband,
which often sends him freely into the doghouse to
get out of the chicken coop. Although double occu-
pancy with Rover can be a tight squeeze, under the
circumstances it's often quieter and safer.

Horsefeathers
On the day Pegasus got a little too frisky and flew
his master too close to the sun, Zeus decided it
wasn't a good idea to let horses be born with wings
any more. He couldn't have his riders coming back
with singed eyebrows. So he grounded his steeds by

taking away all their horsefeathers, saying that he would have no such nonsense going on. Ever since "horsefeathers" has been an expression used to retort to any folly or foolishness.

Horse Sense
What Zeus gave horses after taking away their feathers and what we say about people who appear to be grounded and demonstrate common sense.

A Little Birdie Told Me
Birds, throughout time, have been thought of as messengers of the gods bearing news, as well as carriers of portents and omens. Everyone knows that if you see an owl someone will be sick or die soon—unless a bluebird of happiness follows right behind it, which then cancels out any bad luck. Or this means that you choose to use a carrier pigeon service instead of Ma Bell.

To Goose
Geese can be fairly ferocious beasts and are frequently employed as watchdogs. If you see a goose running at you with head lowered, neck stretched out, and beady little eyes trained on your gluteus maximus, you'd better shake your gluteus minimus and get out of there. Or you will get to experience the true meaning of lockjaw—the goose's jaw locked onto your now-tweaked cheek. The figurative translation has to do with a not quite as exciting pinch on the derriere given by anyone other than a goose.

Goose Bumps
The pinched, black-and-blue welts of skin that arise on a bitten person after being accosted by a mad goose. The little bumps that arise on the skin of a

goose after being accosted and plucked by a bitten and now mad person. Or what human skin resembles when we get cold or scared.

Let Sleeping Dogs Lie

At first glance this may seem to be a quaint way of hinting that one should be kind and not wake one of God's serenely sleeping creatures. In fact, however, it would be more accurate to compare this innocent caution with suggesting something like "Don't wash behind your ears with sulfuric acid." Both these things could be hazardous to your health. The expression actually means that one should not stir up unnecessary trouble and should leave well enough alone. If you doubt the wisdom in this simplicity, just ask any walking mail carriers.

Guinea Pig

This little rodent isn't a pig and doesn't come from Guinea, West Africa. It originates in Brazil and looks more like a cross between a squirrel and a mouse. I propose a more appropriate name for it: squose. But then, if there were only squoses (or squice), scientists wouldn't have any more guinea pigs to use in their research. And we wouldn't have the expression, which means to use someone for an experiment. But who am I to tamper with the importance of science and the English language? Maybe I better let sleeping guinea pigs lie.

I Smell a Rat

This confers the ability to sense intuitively that something is wrong or underhanded. It also implies that you suspect dishonesty in a person. James Cagney had a more specific and straightforward expression for this type of human vermin: "you dirty rat." Of course, symbolically speaking, a dirty rat (someone who is corrupted) is supposed to be particularly foul smelling and is therefore easy to detect. Or, unsymbolically speaking, you have a two-week-old dead rat somewhere in your house. In this case no ESP is required—just a passably functioning proboscis.

To Lock Horns

If you have ever seen two fully grown antlered bucks dueling it out and felt the ground shake as they pace off, charge, and smash heads, you have a pretty good idea of what locking horns means. If the only wilds you've experienced are the cement-jungle kind, think of this expression in terms of two fully-grown, mean cabdrivers smashing fenders and gesticulating wildly while blowing their horns madly at each other. Either way, you'll get the general idea of how this expression has come to be applied to any violent clash of wills.

Epilogue

Well, my book is done. And my little puppy isn't so little anymore. She'll be a year old in a few months. I've had plenty of time to think about how interesting it's all been. I find it curious how life usually gets you right where you want to be if you'll just get out of the way. At least that has been true for me.

As with all things we come to love—a person, place, or thing—once it becomes part of our life, we can't imagine it not being there. This is certainly the case with my blustery puppy. We have our high times, playing and laughing like two hysterical hyenas in the morning before I'm off to work. We've had our low times—she jumping out of my car on a busy highway while I was trying to change a flat during a pounding rainstorm. Through it all, my life has been much richer for her company.

While I'd like to think that this book has entertained you, I truly hope it has served to remind you of the wonders of the love for a pet—and that it will inspire you to share your life with one. Trust me, it really does make your world a better place.

Karen Webster heads her own consulting firm, Creative Resources, located in Woodbury, Connecticut. Karen's love of animals goes back to her childhood and her first job as a veterinarian's assistant. She has never outgrown her interest in and fondness for human's best friend.